No Chimp Left Behind

an Explanication of the Presidential Origin of the Speechities

D1303972

by Cassandra Sagan

Illustrations by Winky Wheeler

HELICON WEST

San Francisco ~ Seattle

No Chimp Left Behind
© 2004 Cassandra Sagan
Illustrations: Winky Wheeler
Cover design: debi lee mandel
Book design: Christian Brophi

Library of Congress Cataloging-in-Publication Data

Sagan, Cassandra
        No Chimp Left Behind:
        An Explanication Of The Presidential Origin Of The Speechities

ISBN 1-882550-46-3

Printed in the U.S.A.

FIRST EDITION

10 9 8 7 6 5 4 3 2 1

Address all correspondence to:

HELICON WEST
Northwest Distribution Office
5346 235th Avenue, South
Issaquah, WA 98029

Author Disclaimer:

I do not really think that the president is a hairless chimp.
I don't even think he's that funny.

Acknowledgements:

I couldn't have brought this book to fruition without the encouragement and *noodging* of my friends and family, and I would like to extend my grateful thanks to them: Gwen Thomas for the title, Tasha Harmon for sustenance, Shelly Siegel, Penelope St. Claire, Mona Warner, Ryc Williamson, "Pamchela" Sloper, Mark Gallagher, Rivkah Coburn, John-Paul McMullen, Eliana Fromer, Rabbi Aryeh and Beth Hirschfield and everyone at P'nai Or, buddy and proofreader Terri Grayum, Karen Braucher, Roger Tobin, and my kids Aura and Lance Aryeff and Soren Goodman, just to name a few. I would also like to thank the following people: Albert Kaufman, networker extraordinaire, who might be the reason you have this book in your hands; my sister debi lee mandel (www.catsprite.com), who took on the jobs of art adviser, cover designer/artist, and copy editor; Philip Hamilton, who edited the manuscript; and Winky Wheeler (www.WhimsicalPlanet.com), who has been an absolute joy to work with. I was, as well, inspired by Bill Feldspar, Rich and Alex's website www.bushorchimp.com, Thom McNichol's essay "Bushonics Speakers Strike Back," and *Super, Duper Monkey*, written by third-grade student Brittney. Thanks to Jacob Weisberg of *Slate* for his postings and three editions of "George W. Bushisms," Robert S. Brown for his books and calendars, "Presidential *(Mis)*Speak: The Very Curious Language of George W. Bush," Al Franken, Michael Moore, Molly Ivins, Jim Hightower, Tom Tomorrow and everyone who can still make me laugh while informing me about the state of the union, along with Michael Parenti, MoveOn.org, *Tikkun Magazine*, and the ones who tell it like it is without the jokes. And for my beloved Bruce Morris, the most generous person I've ever known.

To each of you, I say: uphold the language, and **get out the vote!**

Cassandra Sagan
Portland, Oregon
January 2004

CONTENTS

Actual quotes from President George W. Bush are in bold face.

CHAPTER ONE
THE PRESS CONFERENCE

"Kawazaki?"

"Kawas*niewski*," repeated the President's Speech and Language advisor for what felt like the seventieth time. "The press conference begins in five minutes. Let's take it slowly: Kaw—"

"Look, can't I just call him President 'C' and leave alone what is well enough?"

Dan Matt turned helplessly to the press secretary, Gail Reese, and threw his hands in the air. "Can't we say he has laryngitis?"

Gail frowned. "Not again. It's too soon." She stood up, tilted her chin in a determined fashion. "Leave this to me."

*

President Victor Vincent Thorn, dubbed "Double V" by friend and foe alike, was well known for his difficulty with the pronunciation of foreign names and the construction of basic, complete sentences and thoughts. But few were aware of the enormous effort the administration made to control the potential damage of Double V's blundering efforts. They employed a full-time Speech and

Language advisor, or S&L man, to prep him on pronunciation, subject-verb agreement, and basic usage before all public speaking events. When he wasn't hiding in an undisclosed location or recovering from heart failure, the Vice President addressed the press. They hired a staff and cabinet of people with exclusively monosyllabic names. A highly skilled PR intervention crew was sought and trained.

Despite their best efforts, everyone on the planet was aware of Double V's linguistic incompetence. But there was only one human being on Earth who knew the real reason behind the President's misuse of the English language.

*

"Dan, let's find a little wall with a hole in it after the hoohoohaha is finished and the past is in front of ourselves, and have a couple or two of them sweet banana decrees," suggested Double V, fiddling energetically with his tie as if it were trying to strangle him.

"*Daiquiris*," groaned Dan, head in hands.

"That sounds like a yes!" grinned the President.

"NO!" Dan spat. "You're on the wagon, Victor."

"Wagons that aren't moving can't keep folks from falling off," said Double V. "Howzabout a banana spit then?"

"SPLIT!"

"Don't you think I'd be at a misadvantage if I split right before the press conference is over or beginning to start?"

Gail Reese raced back into the room. "I've worked it out with the sound man. Here's the plan: Victor, whenever you're about to say President Kawasniewski's name, I want you to lead up to it slowly with a long list of adjectives. The sound man will know what's coming and distort the microphones just long enough for you to mispronounce . . . I mean *say*, Kawasniewski."

"Now, uh, just what is *objectives*?" He scratched his head in a manner people had found endearing ever since his youngest days.

The S&L man cut in. "*Adjective*. A word that modifies a noun, gives you a little more information, describes the quantity or qualities of a person, place, or thing."

Double V began to jump up and down, a behavior he often displayed when he grasped a difficult concept.

"Like yellow? A yellow banana?"

"Yes. Yellow is an adjective."

Double V began to jump up and down, a behavior he often displayed when he grasped a difficult concept.

"Like slimy, yellow banana?" he crooned.

Dan, encouraged by the President's success, nodded his head.

"Long, slimy, yellow banana?"

Gail Reese pushed Dan aside.

"Mr. President! One minute until the press conference begins. You need to use adjectives that describe Aleksander Kwasniewski, the President of Poland, not adjectives that describe a banana. Try saying 'my esteemed colleague, the caring and intelligent President. . . .' and then you keep talking, but the sound will be fuzzy."

Double V began to laugh, his distinctive "eeee, eeee, eeee," that his aids generally tried to prevent the public from hearing. "Eeeee, eeeee, eeee, I like calling things 'fuzzy'!"

*

The press conference was held in the Presidential Palace, a Baroque-style mansion in Warsaw. Although President Thorn stepped up to the microphone with his big, oft-charming grin, the crowd that faced him wasn't smiling back. News reporters and concerned citizens hurled questions at him, each louder and angrier than the last.

"Mr. President! On what basis are you willing to deploy a missile defense system that violates the basic tenets of the 1972 Anti-Ballistic Missile treaty?"

"I don't want nations feeling like that they can bully ourselves and our allies. I want to have a ballistic defense system so that we can make the world more peaceful, and at the same time I want to reduce our own nuclear capacities to the level commiserate with keeping the peace. We cannot let terrorists and rogue nations hold this nation hostile or hold our allies hostile. We'll let our friends be the peacekeepers and the great country called America will be the pacemakers."

"President Thorn, how do you defend your rejection of the Kyoto Protocol?" shouted another reporter.

"First, we would not accept a treaty that would not have been ratified, nor a treaty that I thought made sense for the country."

"Whatever happened to that bipartisan cabinet you promised? And what is your plan to limit greenhouse gas emissions that virtually every scientist who is not hired by big oil companies says contribute to global warming?"

"Now, whoa, whoa, whoa! That's Texas for 'hold your horse'! I came here to welcome Poland to NATO, and if that isn't what I'm gonna do then I don't know what is."

He cleared his throat and continued. "So, it's obvious that NATO, the North American . . . No. North Alabama? Apple? Well, it's oblivious that NATO and all the fine things those four powerful letters abbreviate will be of great benefit from the emission of you strong-mouthed Polandians to our prideful ranks. Like I was telling President 'C' . . . I mean, my um, steamed, yellow college President Kaw . . ."—the sound through the PA system went temporarily fuzzy —". . . that with all these nice people joining NATO, and maybe even being united as one nation with other Europeans, our friends in **Russia should not fear the expansion of peace-loving people to her borders**. Just because the Soviet Union fell apart once doesn't mean it will again."

From across the room Gail Reese slid her hand sharply in front of her neck as if she were attempting to sever her own head. Victor tried to remember what that signal meant.

"Don't misunderestimate me," he winked. **"We're making the right decisions to bring the solution to an end."**

*

Later that night, Dan Matt and Gail Reese sat side by side in a corner of a darkened pub, mumbling into their Smirnoff's. Dan said, "Not only that, Thorn actually said: **'I'm so thankful, and so gracious—I'm gracious that my brother Jab is concerned about the hemisphere as well.'** I can't believe I left a tenure-track position in the Linguistics department at Columbia to work with a . . . a man with the speech habits and mental capacity of a primate. Give me an actor like Raygun who works off his script any time. Day after day listening to the President of the United States abusing what I hold most dear, catching the sacred butterfly of language and pulling off its legs and antennae, tugging at the wings . . . ." Dan wiped away a tear. "I've dedicated my life to the preservation of literary culture. Sometimes it's more than I can bear."

*

Little did Gail or Dan, or anyone else in the Republican Party know, that other, more ancient interests were using Victor Vincent Thorn as a puppet, and to even greater effect.

CHAPTER TWO
A BRIEF HISTORY OF HAIRLESS CHIMPANZEES

In his rhinoskin toga and long, matted hair, hunched to the ground with his arms swinging, garlanded with thick vines and pungent tropical blooms, you might not realize that Envee-vee was human. You might wonder at the thick, brown fur covering his face, hands, and strong, curved back. You might shudder in horror as he slowly, gleefully, dismembered a butterfly.

Envee-vee was the only human being on Earth who knew Double V's true origins.

*

From time beyond memory until the recent past, a chimpanzee born without hair was treated with the same ruthless instinct towards survival as any other physically impaired chimp: abandoned on a mountaintop, exposed to the elements. Life was brutal and short, and if you could not carry your share of the community burden you were left to die with the old and infirm.

Of course, homo sapiens do not have a monopoly on evolution. Since the time 500 million years ago when our common simian ancestor subdivided into chimp, ape, and human families, all the related subspecies have evolved, each at their own pace, in their own way, in response to their particular environment. Although the evolution of the human family has been the most dramatic, the chimpanzee runs a close second. Over millennia, chimps developed a primitive technology, employing rocks as tools and weapons, grinding and shaping sticks for use as both digging and musical instruments. They developed social structures and hierarchies, and a rudimentary language suitable for communicating simple ideas and information. And deep in their caves and dark, tangled jungles, in the cool shade of endangered trees far from the prying eyes and ears of humans, they received the Gift of Prophecy and developed the Rituals of Telepathy.

*

Early last century, Oola-la, one of the most sexually popular chimps in the community, was in the throes of a difficult labor. She clutched at the thick vines, twenty knuckles pale with effort. Several of the elder females, responding to her anguished hoots, gathered to offer support and comfort. Young males, each imagining himself to be the father, offered up a rhythm, beating their kimora sticks against a hollow log. (This rhythm later became popularized as the "Bo Diddley" rhythm after a young American traveling in Africa heard the chimps playing their kimora sticks in the distance.)

The moment the baby chimp was born, the females let out a mournful wail and turned aside in horror. The rhythm of the kimora subsided. For a moment, the jungle was still.

The chimp was hairless.

Shema-ma however, did not turn away, even when she heard the mourning cry of the other elders, even as she felt the silence. She was completely blind now, but because she had once been the most sexually popular and was mother and grandmother to many, no one had left her yet to die.

Suddenly a trembling came upon her, as if she were the one who had just given birth. Her fur stood straight out; she bolted completely upright as if walking through tall grass. Several chimps later reported seeing sparks of electricity fly off her body. Shema-ma held up two fingers on each hand forming

"And at the turn of the century one of these undead chimps what don't have any hair will become the powermost person on the world."

what were at the time mistaken for peace signs, but retrospectively understood as two Vs.

It was the time of the First Prophecy.

"Deathifying of unhaired chimps is unpermissioned and inacceptable! We some day being salvationed by a chimp who hasn't got hair not none not any!" She bellowed in a voice strangely hoarse and deep. It seemed to come through her, like music through a hollow reed, as if the forest itself were speaking. Every chimp in earshot recognized the power of the moment and listened breathlessly.

"This law must be forcedly enstrict. Murderation will be untolerated nor will we stand for it. Not never." Her entire body began to vibrate as if she were on a twenty-five cent pony ride in front of a Kmart.

"Though these non-hairful chimps fills us with disgustment and we don't even like it, they assemble human beings.

"They will live among humans.

"And at the turn of the century one of these undead chimps who don't have any hair will become the powermost person on the world.

"This chimp will be named Vee-vee."

And with that Shema-ma collapsed to the ground, dead.

The birds commenced to peck and twitter, the insects to hum, the wind to rattle the branches.

Oola-la held her newborn to her breast.

CHAPTER THREE
THE CHIMPS' AGENDA

The clan that prepared for the coming of the hairless messiah was a renegade band of misfits, artists, and politicos. Some were escapees from Jane Goodall's primate sanctuary. Several had appeared on *Wild Kingdom*. Many had parents and grandparents incarcerated in metropolitan zoos. Others were descended from chimps who had been led cruelly by fate into laboratories where products were tested for human use. One had actually been featured in an advertising campaign for stain-resistant carpeting, another had appeared several times on *Letterman*. Most had lost loved ones to hunters of exotic game.

Though their talents and backgrounds varied significantly, they agreed on one point: their utter disdain for the human side of the family.

Ever more deeply they penetrated the jungle, settling farther and farther from people, their roads and their chainsaws, their greed and their terrifying nets, far from other chimpanzee communities. Their culture evolved in isolation, fueled by bitterness, informed by refugees who regularly joined their ranks.

*

One morning the council gathered as they always did, to pick lice, crush and munch dung beetles, and gripe about the Human Condition.

"Darwin!" spat Oyvey-vey. All present made the raspberry sound. "Like a human wasn't gonna name their own specie as most fittest for survivaling."

"A truthfuller statement wasn't never spoken," another chimp chimed.

"If Darwin were a chimp, then probability he would've selected chimps as the fittingest," said Oyvey-vey.

Everyone gave the four thumbs up in agreement.

"When Vee-vee is born, then we take our rightened places as the least unpowerful specie this planet has ever been caretook by. The humans have done too not good of a job for enough long."

Everyone grunted vigorously, pounding each other on the back. Everyone except Gambo-bo, a refugee from a video game testing lab in Berkeley. He peeled a banana with a sneer of sheer contempt on his face. Because he had endured the longest and most intimate contact with humans, Gambo-bo, ironically, was considered alpha male as well as clan geek.

"I'm sick and awake of you chimps chanting 'Vee-vee, Vee-vee, Vee-vee,' like some hairless chimp is gonna be borned and then like magical become the powerfullest human of Earth," spat Gambo-bo. "You are basking in laziment. If we don't make it happen then the nothing that is happening already will keep on continuing. It's up to we. The future of this planet is in our four hands!"

Oyvey-vey said, "You is not unwrong, my 'panzee!"

"My 'panzee!" everyone chimed in agreement.

Gambo-bo continued. "As you alls know, I have expertness in experimentalizing with not an unfew chemical substances."

"Eeee, eeee, eeee!" Everyone chuckled at the understatement. Gambo-bo was famous for his concoctions, potions, and decompositions of psychoactive agents. He had even harvested and dried a marijuana-like substance and rolled a loose but definite joint; however, since chimps had not yet learned how to start a fire, the joint remained poised behind his ear and ready for inhaling in the event of a lightning storm. Everyone in the community had spent time with Gambo-bo partaking of various formulations, sometimes marveling for hours at the beauty of a single leaf, sometimes puking until they passed out, nursing

"If us is to gain controlship of this planet through Vee-vee, the unhaired one, then us must toil unceasingly so us is ready when he comes."

headaches that throbbed three days and longer. Rumor had it that, back in his California days, captive in a primitive video game lab where programs were developed for training military fighter pilots, some of the interns had whetted his appetite for alternative states of consciousness by dosing him with early, pure strains of LSD.

Gambo-bo continued. "Latently, I've been experimentalizing with a new substance I call 'Blue Manna'." He reached into a hole in the nearest tree and scooped up a handful of iridescent glop. The other chimps scratched their heads in curiosity. Oyvey-vey reached out to touch it; Gambo-bo, horrified, kicked the inquisitive chimp aside.

"Do not misunderestimate the power of Blue Manna," he warned. "I misunderstand how it works, but I know if you touch this you will be inpowered to me. My slave. For internity."

Gambo-bo went on to detail his observations of the strange and powerful properties of Blue Manna and the extensive experimentation he had already done. By ritually smearing Blue Manna on the temples and knuckles of himself and another animal, a subtle though unbreakable telepathic bond was created, leaving the hapless animal completely at Gambo-bo's control and mercy. Quite by accident, he discovered that, through a horrifying and unlikely process of dismembering various winged insects, he was able to manipulate word for word his victim's speech; using jungle vines, flora, and foliage, he was able to control the victim's movements and gestures with the dexterity of a master puppeteer. All the chimps agreed that such a powerful substance must be strictly used to serve the good of the planet. And they all agreed on what 'good' is: the chimps must gain the status of primary caretakers of the Earth, before the jungles and air and water and soil were completely destroyed by the humans.

"If us is to gain controlship of this planet through Vee-vee, the unhaired one, then us must toil unceasingly developing the usages of the Blue Manna and the Rituals of Telepathy so us is ready when he comes. Us calls this mission: 'No Chimp Left Behind'."

"No chimp left behind! No chimp left behind!" the chimps cheered, slapping each other on the behind.

CHAPTER FOUR
BIRTH OF VEE-VEE

Late August, 1946. An open jeep sputtered and lurched across the roadless expanse of the Borno region of Nigeria. Vic and Deedee Thorn, clutching their infant son as if he were a handrail, bounced semi-nauseously in the back seat. Although Deedee was a good-hearted young woman of strong moral fiber, she knew she would never be able to reveal to her husband the real reason behind her insistence on spending their vacation in remote Nigeria.

"Niagra?"

"No, Vic, Nigeria. Western Africa."

He'd thought she was teasing at first, although she wasn't one to tease and, if anything, motherhood had made her more serious. Vic, recently home from the war and studying at Yale, had something a little mellower in mind.

"Well Nunu,"—his pet name for her—"I was thinking more along the lines of fly-fishing on the Colorado River, or riding the train to D.C. and catching a glimpse of Truman, but if that doesn't sound romantic enough for my Nunu, we can always go out to Martha's Vineyard."

Deedee shook her head, folding her arms in a way clearly signifying that Vic's fate had been determined.

Vic tried to tempt Deedee with a litany of ever more exotic places, but her desire to travel to Nigeria prevailed.

She said she'd always had a dream of visiting Africa and was afraid that once young Victor began toddling and the large family they were planning came to be, they'd never have the freedom to travel. She insisted that bringing baby Victor to the place on earth farthest away from Connecticut would establish inside of him a sense of belonging to, and having power over, the greater whole.

"And those poor skinny children," she wept into her hanky. "I want to give them some of my spare change. I want to share bites of my sandwich. I want those desperately impoverished mothers to know that America hasn't forgotten them."

But those were lies. The real reason Deedee Thorn was compelled to travel to innermost Africa was far less altruistic: her firstborn was completely covered with a kind of fur, a fuzzy down as soft as dandelion fluff. Deedee could hardly tell what her own son looked like!

Everyone said that it was a normal, natural condition for newborns, nothing to fret over or be ashamed of, and that within weeks the excess hair would fall off. *Everyone* said it, *all* the time. The nurses in the hospital, her relatives, neighbors, the woman standing in line behind her at the grocery store. Children stared, and not a few burst into tears. She was sick of the barrage of shock and pity and patronizing phrases. In Nigeria, if people pitied her, they would do it in a language she couldn't understand.

And more importantly, in Nigeria flowed the Gongola River and grew the P'lip'li flower that already lived powerfully within her imagination because of a story her black nanny had told her to keep her in line when she was a little girl.

"If you don't wash your hands good and get under the nails," warned Elmira, her voice hushing to a ferocious whisper, "you'll grow fur all over your arms and the only thing that will take it off is soaking in the Gongola River and inhaling the fragrance of the P'lip'li flower at midnight."

"If you don't eat all your liver and spinach you'll grow fur up your back. I'll have to throw you in the Gongola and make you inhale the fragrance of the P'lip'li flower. At the dark of midnight. Owl-hooting, cheetah-springing midnight."

Elmira always embellished the story with a host of terrifying details: boiling rapids, hungry snakes, child-eating ants, rabid beavers, gaping crocodiles.

The young mother was a thoroughly reasonable person, yet she was haunted by the fear that some childhood transgression had resulted in her giving birth to a fur-covered baby. And although it was too late to retrieve the hidden lima beans stuffed into the seat cushions of the harp-backed dining room chairs, or scrub thoroughly behind her own nine-year-old ears, or replace the ace of hearts to the deck that February day when she finally beat her best friend at Old Maid, there was one thing Deedee could do: give her firstborn the cure. Take him to the river. Soak him in the water.

*

Throughout her pregnancy Undee-dee felt certain that the chimp she was carrying was somehow special or chosen. Whatever she was doing—swinging from tree to tree to visit friends, gather fruit, or feel the wind in her fur; using a stone hammer and anvil to crack open the nuts of the oil palm tree, which she craved in the way that human women might crave pickles; dipping for carpenter ants with a narrow wand; or grooming, chattering, and dissing humans with the council—she felt a glow inside of her womb, as if she had swallowed a star. There was a bounce to her step, an exuberant swing to her arms, a lightness to her laughter—eeee, eeee, eeee— that she had not experienced during her other two pregnancies. The other females sensed it too, and surprisingly, no jealousy was aroused or expressed.

And so it came to pass that on the morning of July 6th, just as the sun came up over the tops of the kapok trees and the toucans began to sing, Undee-dee gave birth to a hairless chimp. There followed a long moment of silence during which, as legend goes, the Gongola river ceased to flow, the birds and winged insects paused mid-flight, and a halo-like radiance emanated from Undee-dee's head. And then the forest shuddered with Prophecy as the cry of "Vee-vee" rose up from the lips of every chimp and, legend continues, the very voice of the Earth was heard. The rhythm of the kimora filled the air, joyous hoots and hullabaloo echoed off the tree tops, and the P'lip'li flowers bloomed in a single

She felt a glow inside of her womb, as if she had swallowed a star.

crimson wave. The jungle rocked with celebration until the wee hours of the morning.

Only two chimps failed to join in the brouhaha.

One was Gambo-bo, who quietly added the finishing touches to the cave wall carving depicting the various uses of the Blue Manna and Rituals of Telepathy.

The other was Undee-dee, marveling at the thousand wrinkles in her newborn's pale skin, kissing his opposable thumbs, memorizing every detail. Because in a short amount of time—maybe weeks, perhaps a month or two—her baby would be sent off to live with the humans and rule their world.

CHAPTER FIVE
THE GREAT SWITCHEROO

Sneaking away from the encampment just before midnight did not prove as difficult as Deedee Thorn had anticipated. Vic, knocked into oblivion by a combination of local banana daiquiris and a lively roll in the hay, didn't alter the rhythm of his snoring one iota as she swaddled young Victor and bundled him off into the African night.

The moon was full, and it was easy for Deedee to find her way. She retrieved the small basket she'd purchased at the market—woven with willow wands and sealed with pitch—from behind a jacaranda tree, and headed down to the spot on the Gongola she'd scouted earlier. Reeds grew along the edges, the water ran slow and clean, and P'lip'li flowers bloomed along the banks. She undressed her son, tenderly removing the silver spoon from his fist. Tears of guilt and shame welled up in her eyes as she beheld his fragile, fur-covered body. Desperately she grasped a small tuft of down between her thumb and forefinger, gave one final, fruitless tug. The fur held fast.

Deedee had no idea how long one must soak in the Gongola before its depilatory properties kicked in, so she dunked him once quickly, hopefully, startling young Victor Vincent awake. She held the whimpering baby at arm's length.

"Ssh, ssh, it's okay, it's okay," she said, and gave him a little shake to see if the fur would fall off.

It didn't.

Next, Deedee lowered the infant into the warm water for several minutes, until her arms grew sore and Victor calmed down. Expectantly, she pulled him up; no luck. So she dunked a receiving blanket several times into the river until it was drenched, wrapped him snugly, and set him in the willow basket she had secured to the reeds with a length of hemp. Her watch showed five of midnight. Deedee plucked a bouquet of p'lip'li flowers and lay them in the basket close to the baby's nose. Her lips moved slightly in prayer.

At that exact moment the chimps made their move.

Suddenly the forest came to life around her. Branches creaked, leaves rustled, and rotting banana peels squooshed underfoot. The ground began to rumble and a huge panting sound filled the air. Deedee jumped up in terror, her prayers magnified. "Police!" she called without thinking.

And then the source of the ruckus appeared before her, as if in a dream: dozens of chimpanzees, swinging through the branches, walking on their knuckles, hooting and, it seemed to her, smiling, making their way to the river. Deedee relaxed, smiled too: all her associations with chimps were positive. Perhaps this was part of the magic of the Gongola, a significant part of the story Elmira had failed to reveal to her. Or perhaps it was some sort of full moon chimpanzee ritual; indeed, they seemed almost to be singing.

But when Deedee turned back to the river, the rope had come loose and the basket carrying young Victor was gently, steadily flowing down the Gongola.

Frantically, she plunged into the thick reeds, tearing her way through at the level of savage force mothers sometimes embody when it's time to lift a car off of their child's leg.

She called out, "Mama's coming," and howled a curdling, warlike howl.

Was there a steady rhythm beating in the forest around her, or was that the sound of her own heart?

Not far away, little Victor floated toward the edge of a raging waterfall.

How would she ever explain this to Vic? To her mom? To her hairdresser?

She undressed her son, tenderly removing the silver spoon from his fist.

And then, as if from out of the heavens, a chimp swung into a willow with branches hanging far out over the river, a similar warlike howl issuing forth from her primate lips. Just as the basket with the baby in it was about to plummet over the edge and into the waterfall, it caught momentarily on the edge of a great white bush. The long arm of the chimp reached out an impossible distance from the willow and snatched up the baby as the empty basket plunged into the boiling rapids.

*

The next few minutes were a blur, and because Deedee never told the story to anyone, they took on an increasingly surreal quality, of near-mythic proportion.

In her memory of the event, the long-armed chimp bowed as it handed the baby to her, wrapped in his soggy blanket, sighing, still asleep. It even appeared to Deedee that the chimp had tears in its eyes, and that it moved its lips, gesturing emphatically, as if trying to speak. But all Deedee could make out was "Oo oo, aa aa." The trees, the river, the flowers, even the stars, seemed to waver and undulate as in one of Max Fleischman's Betty Boop cartoons. In the jungle all around her, chimps jumped up and down with excitement.

The baby slept on obliviously, breath shuddering in and out. Tentatively, a sobbing Deedee unwrapped her son in an effort to examine his tiny body for bruises or bites or—God forbid—worse.

"I don't care if he stays covered with fur the rest of his life. I will love him with all my heart. I will do anything for this baby. I will raise my other children to serve him unquestioningly. Please, God, let him be okay."

She removed the receiving blanket.

And gasped. And laughed and cried and hugged the infant to her breast, danced her gratitude among the reeds to the sound of flowing water, surrounded by dancing chimps, the scent of P'lip'li blossoms wafting into the midnight air.

Except for a tiny bit of fuzz on the top of his wrinkled pate, young Victor Vincent Thorn was completely hairless! His temples and the backs of his hands were smeared with an iridescent blue substance; in truth, he had a strange blue glow around him, but Deedee hardly noticed.

From that day forward her gratitude and esteem for chimpanzees was second only to her loyalty to her family. She donated tens of thousands of dollars over the years to Jane Goodall's research work at Gombe. It never bothered her that young Victor somewhat resembled a chimp. In fact, she kind of liked it.

*

"Salivation is came!" hooted the chimps with glee, passing around hollowed coconut shells filled with a fine, aged banana liqueur. Their plan had worked without a hitch.

"Chimps is gonna rule the world! The future am now! The past is in front of ourselves!"

Oyvey-vey made an attempt at stand-up comedy, in which he tried to walk upright but kept slipping and tripping on real and imaginary banana peels.

A trio of pubescent females on the verge of swelling with their first estrus sang chittering harmonies in tribute to Vee-vee. "Not Tee-tee, not Pee-pee, not Cee-cee, not Double 'O,' not Double 'U,'" referring to him as the "unhairiest of they all." The kimora sticks beat their rhythm under the moonlight. Ago-go found a long, smooth, nearly straight branch, and the limbo was invented. Everyone danced and leapt about, making the sign of the double 'V,' sometimes with two hands, sometimes with four. Numerous chimps were conceived that night, some more than once. It was the sort of celebration Disney would have had a ball with.

Meanwhile, in the hollow of an ancient Mufuti tree, Undee-dee and Gambo-bo observed the human infant.

"Him sure are the uncarnation of ugliment," grimaced Undee-dee, delaying her first attempt to nurse the child as long as possible. "In my life that is not unwhole, I'm not seen anything of more ugliness. Not never."

"This human am hairful and covered with it. But the way of him's looking is irreverent," said Gambo-bo, smearing on the Blue Manna, adjusting the cradle of vines with an engineer's precision. "What is mattering is that your little Vee-vee will give us controlship of the untire world."

Undee-dee sighed. "My 'panzee, you is not falsicating what is trueness, but

I still has to raise this human like it were my own onspring."

Gambo-bo looked up from his work for a moment and held Undee-dee affectionately in his gaze. "You will be unforgot in legend and in poemtry. Inflect on that when times get hardened and you feel like you simply can't go off."

Tears streaming down her disgust-puckered face, Undee-dee took the human child to her breast and gave him suck.

CHAPTER SIX
HAIL TO THE CHIEF

President Thorn convened his staff in the meeting room of his suite at the SAS Raddison Hotel in Gothenberg, Sweden, over pineapple juice and coconut cream cookies. The agenda was to revise their strategy for warding off an onslaught of anti-American sentiment directed towards the President by irate Europeans during the short course of his tour. Double V swung nimbly from the chin-up bar, as was his custom during meetings. The set up crew installed such a bar in every hotel room where the President lodged, and for longer visits, an entire jungle gym was erected on the grounds. He insisted these be left behind as tokens of his esteem, a sort of high-end graffiti: "President Victor Vincent Thorn was here." Although his staff attempted not to roll their eyes when he said it, the President claimed that swinging from bars "helped him think more better."

"Why don't I just tell the truth? No one here *shprekinzee* English. It would be more simpler if I simply said: 'I know I promised in my campaign to cut carbon-dioxide omissions, but the coal and oil boys gave muchos buckeroos so no can do. You worry about your environment, and let me worry about mine. What do you think all those lines on the map are for?'"

Double V shifted his weight from one hand to the other, hooking his left foot

The President claimed that swinging from bars
"helped him think more better."

over the bar and arching into a half-gainer, then pausing mid-air. The staff exchanged looks, coughed, shuffled papers. Dan Matt, the Speech and Language advisor, spoke up.

"Victor, most Europeans are bi- or trilingual."

The president was aghast. "Do they *know*?"

The S&L man took a deep breath, counted to seven like his therapist had taught him, and tried again. "They understand English as well as their native language. You have to be very careful what you say. The Europeans understand, and they aren't happy with what you're saying."

Double V marveled at the concept. "How can they know which language they are saying? Misspeaking English is hard enough."

Gail Reese stepped in to keep things on track. "Mr. President, let's get back to our rejection of the Kyoto Protocol, which is arousing great apprehension among the European citizenry. The U.S. is responsible for producing approximately twenty-five percent of the greenhouse gases on the planet, yet we are the only industrialized nation not to sign the accord. How can we allay their anxieties, without actually biting the hands that feed us?"

"Gail, it almost sounds like you are speaking like one of them European bilinguals." Victor scratched his head. "However, I think big issues call for big words. How about antidisestablishmentterrorism? It's a biggie." He stretched his hands apart as if he were playing an accordion, smiling cherubically.

Dan Matt wrestled with his emotions. "Yes you are cute. Yes you are likable. That's what got you the presidency—that, and being a Thorn—but it is not an effective way of operating a government."

"Greenhouse gases?" said Gail, restating the issue as plainly as possible.

"Greenhouses. Like 'em. No plant or flower should be left behind. That's **what America is all about.**"

"Let's go over the voluntary pollution control plan," urged Gail. Back in Texas, when Double V was governor, he had supported such a plan designed by two dozen of the biggest polluters in the state and written into a bill by a lobbyist from the Texas Chemical Council. Years later, precious little had changed environmentally, but the public was easily distracted.

"Well, I think if you say you're going to do something and don't do it,

that's trustworthiness," Thorn said.

A sudden uproar from the street below brought them to the window. A small brass band burst into an off-key rendition of "Hail to the Chief," as a thousand protestors turned simultaneously and dropped their drawers.

"I don't like his policies . . . this is one of the only ways we can show how we feel," a German woman later told reporters, pulling up her khakis and zipping them shut.

"We call this tune 'Hail to the Thief,'" quipped the trumpet player.

Gail Reese whipped out her cell phone, speed-dialed her connection at the AP. "Do not let this get out on the wires," she commanded.

"What an outrage! How insulting! Americans everywhere should take strong issue with this embarrassment," spat Dan Matt.

But Double V leaned out the window, waving and smiling. "Dan, you've got it back asswards, as we say in Texas. You have mistook the situation and also got it wrong. These people are not buying me insults; they're knowledging me as leader! They're saying, 'We are just a bared butt in comparisment to you. We are weak. We bow to you in complete humblety. You are powerful, we are unpowerful. You are alpha, we are alfalfa. You take the high road, we take the low road, and we'll be in Sweden before you.'"

Dan Matt pinched his arm, which was bruised and blue as a heroin addict's. Wasn't this all just a terrible dream? "President Thorn, those people just mooned you."

But the president paid his S&L man no mind. Instead, he blew kisses out the window, reassuring the European people that he would use the power they had invested and acknowledged in him.

CHAPTER SEVEN
VICTOR VINCENT: THE EARLY YEARS

He was a poor student, incapable of following a lesson or stringing together a complete sentence. He thought of math problems hieroglyphically: sometimes the number "6" was a cherry, sometimes a lit bomb; "0" was the moon or a vitamin pill; "1"s were always bananas. He loved sports, excelling at gymnastics and wrestling, and recess was his favorite subject. His room was a mess— underwear rolled into knots and left on window sills and door knobs; dirty cups and dishes sprouting a variety of molds; his mouse and insect collection climbed in and out of cigar boxes, crumpled socks, food wrappers, and milk cartons; the down of several feather pillows collected in corners and open drawers. He ate with his hands, sometimes with his feet, sometimes just leaning into the oatmeal and lapping it up. He threw his food on the floor, slurped up liquids, dribbling them down his chin and neck and wiping his mouth with his sleeve. He would gross-out the neighborhood kids by eating ants, caterpillars, and worms, and he caught flies in his mouth and swallowed them without chewing, even when no one was watching. He stared at the television screen for hours on end, mimicking everything in gesture and voice. He either refused to get into the bathtub, climbing up door jambs, rain gutters, elm trees, and telephone poles to elude his mother and babysitters; or else he dove in with his clothes and cowboy boots on, with firetrucks, water pistols, stuffed animals, pet mice, and homework in tow.

In most respects, Victor Vincent Thorn was a regular kid.

What he lacked in scholarship, cleanliness, and manners, he more than made up for in personality.

Young Victor was a popular, likable kid. From his earliest days he was able not only to laugh at his own mistakes, but also to turn them into comedic opportunities. He was an impersonator extraordinaire, and his uncanny imitations of Clark Gable (*Frankly, my dear, a damn is what I don't give you. So if you want a damn you will have to find some other damn guy.*) and James Cagney (*You dirty rat, you ate my brother, and now it's bath time you dirty rat.*) brought smiles to even the stuffiest teacher's lips. In his high school yearbook, under his senior photo, was the caption: *Most likely to impersonate a President.*

His expert mimicry skills made him hands down the class clown, distracting both students and teachers from even the most basic educational experiences.

In a February 19, 2001 interview with *People* magazine, Mrs. Stankoskawicz, his second grade teacher, recalls: "I remember one Thursday afternoon in the middle of December suddenly realizing: 'dang, it's almost Christmas and we haven't even gotten to 1+1 yet.' That little Thorn was so entertaining. I'd be reading to the children and he'd imitate my smallest gesture with such dexterity, scrambling the words with such wit that, well, I admit now that I found it mildly sexually stimulating.

"Of course the little brat could never pronounce my name properly and called me 'Mrs. Stink.' Time after time after time I'd have him bend over and give him a good whack on the tush with my ruler, but he seemed to like it and eventually I had to stop. The poor kid had a terrible time pronouncing almost everything, and could never get words and names straight. He always referred to our country as 'The Undisconnected States of A Miracle,' so I wasn't too surprised when he referred to it that way during his inaugural address."

Young Victor was always getting himself in trouble, then charming his way out. He was a regular in the principal's office where, minutes after dancing on desktops and swinging from light fixtures, he'd crouch beside the secretaries, placing a pretend pencil behind his ear, typing letters in midair, and then

He'd pick up a banana as if it was a telephone receiver,
then squeeze it into his mouth—pop!

pushing his head carriage-like at the end of a sentence. He'd pick up a banana as if it were a telephone receiver, then squeeze it into his mouth—pop!— swishing it around back and forth between his cheeks then downing it in a single gulp.

The secretaries adored him.

"He had an animal magnetism," reminisces Bev Jones, one of Thorn's elementary school secretaries, in an April 2001 interview. "He wasn't like the other kids."

From his earliest days he was able not only to laugh at his own mistakes, but also to turn them into comedic opportunities.

Young Victor was adept at employing his wit and charm toward self-preservation. Paul Wolf, former school bully who now serves as Deputy Secretary of Defense under Thorn, said: "I just wanted to knock that goofy grin off his face. But something would come over me, you know, he'd swing his skinny arm around and around like a wobbly propeller or something and pretend like he was gonna wallop me, and my fist would just sort of dangle mid-air. It's impossible to beat the guy." Wolf was one of the few people to join Thorn's cabinet willing to shorten his name.

Young Victor was very close to his mother. Perhaps that is why in later years he was quoted as saying, **"Republicans understand the importance of bondage between mother and child."** Their strongest bond was their mutual love for chimpanzees and all creatures primate.

Many pleasant hours were spent snuggling on the sofa, mesmerized by episodes of *Wild Kingdom*. Victor loved the Curious George books so much that Vic the Elder joked that they were more important to his son than the Bible. Young Victor would stare at the illustrations as if he were trying to memorize them. If he had an upset stomach, readings of Curious George seemed to soothe him. Victor often wished that his name was George.

Young Victor and Deedee would spend delightful hours at the movie theater watching *Monkey Business* and *Monkey's Uncle*. Their favorite, of course, was *Bedtime for Bonzo*. Years later, when Vic the Elder served as Vice-President under *Bonzo*'s leading man, Victor Vincent would greet the President by asking after Bonzo. "Eeee, eeee, eeee," they'd laugh together.

He loved *Dr. Doolittle* and *Animal Farm*, but his favorite book was *Super, Duper Monkey*, written and illustrated by Brittney, when they were classmates in the third grade. It was the story of a monkey who dreamed of speaking with the humans. One night, the monkey snuck away from the jungle and, despite great perils, made his way to the Big City. There, he found some human beings, but when he tried to talk to them all that came out was "Oo oo, aa aa."

"You poor thing," said one kind woman, realizing that Super Duper Monkey was trying to communicate. She took him home and taught him how to talk, and from that day forward he was able to speak to both humans and monkeys. Victor Vincent loved the book so much that Brittney gave him her only copy of it for Valentine's Day. At times when Victor was struggling with his Language Arts homework, or rather, when his English teachers were struggling with him, Deedee wished *Super, Duper Monkey* was a true story and that she could find that kind woman and pay her to teach Victor how to talk properly.

Sometimes mother and son would stroll through the city zoo for hours on end, returning to the monkey house with peanuts, fruit, popcorn, and cameras. At least a dozen times Deedee turned away for what felt like a single moment, only to find young Victor shimmying up the outside bars of one of the cages. The animals seemed genuinely fond of him, too, reaching through the bars not with greed as they usually did, but with a sort of curiosity and fondness.

"Oo oo aa aa," they would call out to him, and young Victor would respond, "Oo oo aa aa," and the monkeys, the baboons, the gorillas, the chimps, the orangutans all seemed to nod in agreement. Often Deedee had to pull him away from what appeared to be enthusiastic conversations.

"That's impossible!" thought Deedee. After all, she was a reasonable woman.

So she decided to prove to herself the ridiculousness of the notion one day when no one was in earshot. "Oo oo aa aa," she called in greeting.

The monkeys stared at her blankly.

"Oo oo aa aa," she repeated with more volume.

They made uncomprehending faces, shrugged their palms skyward, and turned back to a lively discussion they were having with Victor.

"Mommy, me wanna be a zoo man when me grow up."

"But honey, all zookeepers really do is clean up monkey doo-doo," said Deedee, grimacing.

"I know!" laughed Victor, jumping up and down. "And elephant doo-doo and tiger doo-doo and snake doo-doo and giraffe doo-doo and lion doo-doo. All the aminal doo-doo! Can me, please?"

Deedee was certain that Victor's fascination with chimps, even his remarkable physical agility, stemmed from the fact that a chimpanzee had saved his life. How could such a miracle not make a profound impact on an infant's development? At times Deedee found herself thinking that her son somewhat resembled a chimp. But she shook her head, laughing. "Every mother thinks her child is beautiful."

CHAPTER EIGHT
THE STUDENT COUNCIL ELECTION

Perhaps Vic the Elder had a few too many the night he sat his older boys down and demanded that they go into politics. He wanted to start immediately by setting Vincent up as Student Council President. "I'm gearing up for a run at the U.S. House of Reps and I need to start my campaign right here at home. The more Thorns we have in office, the more decisions we can make in the interest of our supporters in the oil industry. I want to put a Thorn in every side!"

"But Dad," said Nill, "teenagers can't be persuaded by oil interests! It's the early '60s. The only teenagers who have their own cars are in the movies, like James Dean, except he's dead."

"Well, it's time you boys had your own cars and set a standard for American families to own as many cars as possible. I guess we'll need a four- or five-car garage. I'll hire some Mexican kids at two dollars an hour to build one, smack dab in front of the house in plain view for all to envy and strive to achieve."

"But Dad," said Jab, "Nill and I are too young to drive, and Victor has flunked Drivers Ed twice."

Vic reached for his wallet. "Well, that won't happen again. Victor, we'll get you your license and a nice big gas hogmobile—a red convertible—and you'll be waving and grinning and elected Student Council President in no time. The earlier the American people start voting Republican the better. Few people in this society ever mature beyond their teenage sensibilities, and I want to capitalize on that trend."

"But Dad, high school politics aren't organized along party lines," noted Nill. He didn't really want the responsibility of political life. He was hoping to live comfortably off his trust fund and spend his time playing the horses, the stock market, and a little bit of blues banjo. Jab wasn't interested in politics either. He was hoping to be a used car salesman when he grew up.

"I wanna be a zoo man!" said Victor, jumping on the sofa.

"Well you are not going to be a zoo man!" spat Vic the Elder. "All you boys are going into politics. I want the Thorn name to be synonymous with power. I want politics to be covered with Thorns. When the American people think of Republicans I want them to think of Thorns. When they think of government I want them to think Thorns. And starting with the Main High School Student Council elections, Thorn equals President."

"Listen, Dad, Victor is popular and all, but that Hal Bore who's already running is a shoo-in. He was vice president last year, and he's actually, well, really smart. He's president of the debate team. He's a master debater."

Vic shrugged off the information. "How big is Bore's media budget?"

The boys looked at each other. "I doubt that he has one," said Jab.

"We're in like Flynn!" laughed Vic. "We'll start with full-page ads in the Sunday paper and thirty-second commercial spots during *Gidget*. My big oil cronies both here and in Saudi Arabia have already dumped thousands into my campaign war chest. I'm sure that funneling a little into the next generation won't upset anyone."

Victor wrestled with the strong, conflicting emotions that roiled inside of him. He wanted nothing more in this life than to please Dad, and the idea of running for president seemed to fulfill a deep sense of destiny. Yet something was really bothering him.

"But Dad . . ." he started.

"Don't 'but Dad' me," commanded Vic the Elder.

"Okay, Dad, but, *yellow*," said Victor.

"Yellow?" frowned Vic. "I don't understand."

"Not red! I want a yellow invertible. Please?"

*

Despite Victor's extravagant campaign financing and exotic platform, Hal Bore commanded a significant lead in the polls. Simply put, Bore made sense and Thorn did not.

"I promise if selected I will smallen the size of the student government and give the control back to the persons," said Victor, grinning at the lectern, raising his arms in the air. The other Thorn boys, as well as a handful of students whose fathers were in oil, clapped uproariously.

"But that's preposterous," countered Hal Bore, pushing his spectacles up his nose. "Student government *is* the way we as teenagers get any control at all. If we limit the size and power of student government, then all the power goes back into the hands of our parents and teachers." The rest of the student body howled in agreement.

"What I am against," said Thorn, **"is grades. I am against hard grades, grades they basically delineate based upon whatever. However they delineate, grades, I think vulcanize society. So I don't know how that fits into what everybody else is saying, their relative positions, but that's my position.** When I am selected president, everyone will get straight 'A's. I think kids are **more likely to succeed with success as opposed to failure."**

There was an enthusiastic thundering of applause.

"Thorn proposes to cut out the very heart of America, the fundaments of our beloved system of competition by which every American can strive to perfect himself and come out on top! What success is possible without effort? If Thorn gets his way, we'll be a school of underachievers, lazy illiterates, staring at our report cards instead of studying and learning so that we might devote ourselves to making this nation the greatest that has ever been."

A lot of students applauded, but not everyone. Straight "A"s sounded good, but . . .

"Bore," cried Thorn, shaking his head, "that is some fuzzy thinking you are evolved in. Straight 'A's is straight 'A's no matter what side of the deck you have

"The fact that he relies on facts—says things that are not factual—are going to undermine his campaign."

dealt them from. **The fact that he relies on facts—says things that are not factual—are going to undermine his campaign."**

Cheers followed, accompanied by a low hum of hisses.

"When I am nominated to president, I promise that every student which goes to Main High will get his or she's own car!" continued Thorn, thumping his fist enthusiastically on the podium.

"What a ridiculous promise!" frowned Bore. "My worthy opponent may as well promise you each a trip to the moon. I, however, promise that if elected I will see to it that seniors with a "B" average or higher will earn the privilege of chewing gum in the cafeteria!"

"Hey kids, you choose—" countered Thorn, "—Bazooka, or Buick? When selected, I will inappropriate funds to purchase the three-acre emptied lot next to the factuality parking lot. It will become the student parking lot and I guess we'll need something to put in it. If we build it, they will come."

Bore smirked. "I guess this is what you call 'getting the bull by the Thorns.'" The bright kids chuckled.

Thorn continued. "So morefurther, when you select me president, I have promises from the local car dealship boys that every kid what goes to Main High will get sweet credit lines. So you can get a cool car and not have to finish paying for it until after you gravitate from college!"

Amanda Heller, the math whiz, shouted out, "But if we do that we'll end up paying three or more times what the car is worth. We'd be selling our futures!"

Young Thorn laughed, "Debt *is* the future of America! Why let everyone else eat the pie when you can have more than your share now? **I think we should make the pie higher."**

*

The Thorn boys gave away dozens of yellow T-shirts inscribed with the campaign slogan "BAZOOKA OR BUICK? VOTE THORN!" and "FEELING THORNY?" They drove through the neighborhoods in the yellow convertible while Victor waved, Nill played blues banjo, and Jab passed out banana splits. They ran a full-page color ad in the Sunday paper depicting the entire student body driving sporty cars on the moon, chewing fat wads of gum, and waving report cards with straight "A"s, while a dour-faced Hal Bore watched through binoculars from a distant campus on Earth.

Nonetheless, on election day, despite the fact that his campaign slogan was "Stay Bored!" the sensible Hal Bore was ahead in the polls by a wide margin.

So Jab and Nill had no choice but to put Plan "B" into action.

As the votes were cast during fifth period and the student council deputies made ready to gather and tally the ballots, the fire alarm went off. As everyone grumbled towards the exits, they noticed smoke pouring out from under the door of the boys' bathroom and chaos broke loose. Teenagers raging with hormones panicked and screamed, ran back to rescue science projects, love letters, and leather jackets; teachers blew whistles in an attempt to herd everyone safely out of the building. The big red fire engine screeched up to the front of the school, the hoses were unrolled and, although the small paper fire was already out, the firemen hosed the bathroom down just to err on the side of caution.

Meanwhile, Jab and Nill snuck into the accelerated English and Trigonometry classrooms, hotbeds of Bore support, and removed the ballots.

The election results were a little anti-climactic after all the excitement: Thorn 470, Bore 452. Victor got on Jab's shoulders and they pranced victoriously through the corridors.

Hal Bore was in the middle of his concession speech when the sheer mathematics of it hit him like a ton of butterflies. "And so I concede the election to my worthy opponent. . . hey, wait a minute! 470 plus 452 adds up to 922, and there are 1,006 students at this school. I demand a recount!"

Principal Hardly agreed that the numbers were off and declared the results inconclusive. But a recount, overseen by supporters of both candidates, bore the same results.

"Something is rotten in Denmark," scowled Bore. "There are votes missing! Something happened during that little 'fire drill'. I demand a revote!"

Arguments and accusations were hurled from side to side. "He's just being a sore loser," said Thorn.

"And he's trying to steal the election," replied Bore.

It went to the student council, but they were evenly split. Eventually, Principal Hardly and Vice Principal Laurel had to decide whether or not to allow a revote.

"Bottom line," said Hardly. "Vic Thorn was president of the school board when I was hired. He got me in on a technicality, despite that little episode back in '58."

Laurel nodded. "My brother-in-law and Vic have been in business together for years."

There was a long pause, pregnant as a chad, round as a loophole.

"It wouldn't be fair to the kids who already voted. It would unjustly penalize students who might be absent that day. It's past the deadline for the votes to have been counted. If we allow a revote we'll have to allow revotes clear back to the founding of this high school in 1907. The election results remain valid."

*

And so it came to pass that Victor Vincent Thorn was elected president of the Main High School Student Council.

Hal Bore went on to be a highly respected environmental lawyer and never tried his hand at politics again.

CHAPTER NINE
IS OUR CHILDREN LEARNING?

"The first thing you have to remember," counseled Vic the Elder, "is: act like you've got a mandate."

Double V, swinging from the bar that workmen had recently installed in the Oval Office, stared at his father in shock.

"But, Dad, a *man*date! I don't go out with men. I'm married."

Dan Matt, the newly appointed Speech and Language Advisor, stepped in. "Mr. President, a mandate would mean that you received a large percentage of the votes and interpret that as the voice of the people demanding that we enact fully our most conservative agenda."

"In other words, Boy, we'll do whatever we damn well please," grinned Vic the Elder. "Who's going to stop us? The Democrats no longer have a cohesive moral or political view. We've rendered them incapable of appealing to their own constituencies. They're all moderate Republicans wearing *papier mâché* donkey ears, measuring their efficacy in capitalistic, conservative terms—*our* terms. The American people are stressed out, overworked, and disenchanted; they won't stop you. If they don't like what you're doing, they'll just change the channel. Our boys own and operate most of the networks anyway. And Lord knows I handpicked half the Supreme Court myself, and they handpicked you.

Go forth and rule the world."

"So then it's okay to paint the White House yellow?" crooned Victor.

"Negative!" piped in Gail Reese, press secretary. "We've been through this, Sir. We can't mess with the sacred cow."

"Then let's change the cow to a monkey and paint 'em both yellow."

As a compromise on the interior decorating front, the Rose Room was redone in a jungle motif reminiscent of Max's bedroom in *Where The Wild Things Are*. And as Victor Vincent Thorn's first act as President of the United States of America, he ordered a complex system of monkey bars to be erected on the White House grounds, visible from both the Oval Office and the Jungle Room, so that he could view Americans deriving the immediate benefits of his administration. "This is the most best thing to happen to the body of the American people since JKF's Physical Fittest Pogrom," he announced to the press.

*

It was decided by the Grand Ol' Poobahs that Double V should focus a lot of media attention on education, to counteract the impression made by his bumbling speech that he was only marginally literate.

"I am not illegitimate," declared the President, mightily offended. "My parents knew each other in the biblical sense. They definitely had sex before they had me."

He continued. "Education cannot be overvalued enough. **The public education system in America is where children learn to take advantage of our fantastic opportunistic society.** The impotence of a good education will last a lifetime or longer. I myself have been educated to a surprising degree—an MBA from Yale!"

*

The agenda of the Grand Ol' Poobahs was simple: keep as much money as possible circulating through the hands of the richest one percent. Developing an educational plan aimed at achieving these goals required that children have their creativity and spirit educated out of them so that they would be left feeling powerless and unsatisfied, floundering in a meaningless void where the only cure and comfort is to consume more goods. They called this plan, "No child left behind."

On the other hand, Double V, by virtue of his manipulation by Gambo-bo and the chimps through the Blue Manna and the Rituals of Telepathy, was a pawn of the chimpanzee agenda, as well. Their goal was to annihilate, or at least render subservient, the human species, which, although quite different from the Poobah's agenda, was addressed via remarkably similar means: create an emotional and spiritual vacuum in which the human race would self-destruct by engaging their basest instincts and wind up shopping to death. They called this plan, "No chimp left behind."

*

At first Victor was opposed to focusing on literacy. **"It just doesn't resignate with me,"** he said.

But then a voice that welled up from deep inside of him—the voice of Gambo-bo—directed his impulses.

"Rarely is the question asked: 'Is our children learning?'" He addressed a teachers' conference in South Carolina. "Well, is they? I will not stand **for the subsidation of failure**. If our children fail, then they aren't going to do very good. If our children isn't learning, then it's because we isn't teaching. **Reading is the basics for all learning. You teach a child to read, and he or her will be able to pass a literacy test. Then America will be a literate country, and a hopefuller country."**

He advocated for accountability reform in education, calling for a rigorous series of standardized tests to be given nationally at each grade level. The teachers' union protested vigorously, although their objections never made it to the Poobah-owned mainstream media.

"When we teach to the test, our creativity and viability in the classroom are totally usurped," they complained.

"You teach a child to read, and he or her will be able to pass a literacy test."

"Don't teach to the test," responded Double V. "Teach to the children."

And to the children he said, **"When your teachers say, 'read'—you ought to listen to her.** Of course I read. **I read the newspaper.** Although CNN and Fox News is easier. "

Briefly, the President made a show of visiting schools, going right into classrooms and pulling adorable, impoverished youngsters onto his lap. He encouraged them with such wisdom as, "Reading will make you less stupider" and "Learning will **embetter** your life."

"This is Preservation Month. I appreciate preservation. It's what you do when you run for President. You gotta preserve," Double V told a group of fourth graders at Fairgrounds Elementary School to help kick off their Perseverance Month assembly.

*

Back in the Borno region, Gambo-bo grew impatient. "School reformication is too unfast," he complained to the council one morning. "At the rate us is moving, the kids schooled now willn't be destroying human culture for years to come. Us needs to move quick along some fronts which are not this one."

"You is unmistaken in your 'ception, as alway, my 'panzee," agreed the chimps, somber and focused on the manifestation of their life work, their *raison d'être*. They put their heads together and began to delineate their next avenues of attack.

Meanwhile, a stone's throw away, Envee-vee listened in on the council with a smirk, dismembering winged insects and formulating his own plan: to escape this moldy paradise, speak directly to human beings, take up his birthright, and rule the world.

CHAPTER TEN
NATURE OR NURTURE?

Devolution is much slower than evolution. Devolution involves building a six-story brick building—designing a blueprint, laying the foundation, framing the internal structure, setting bricks and spreading mortar; adding a roof, wiring, dry wall, windows, and so on and so forth—and then disassembling it in reverse order, until all that is left are piles of materials. Destruction, i.e., taking a bundle of dynamite and blasting the building to high holy heaven, is another story altogether. So it is not surprising that Vee-vee, known to the rest of the world as Double V, managed to accelerate most of five million years of evolution into a single lifetime, while Envee-vee barely devolved at all.

Ol , sure, Envee-vee's pelvis had elongated and he knuckle-walked more often than not; he had developed moderately opposable big toes, and the dusting of "newborn" fluff had never fallen off, turning a rich, dark brown over the years. He had many of the habits of a chimpanzee: he slept in tree nests that he built anew each night; he drank, not from cups, but by squeezing the moisture out of leaf clusters; he considered grubs, carpenter ants, and termites culinary delicacies; and expressed attraction for members of the opposite sex by leaning back and humping the air while pant-hooting, although, invariably, the females swung away in disgust.

But Envee-vee still had a human heart. He was able to observe the human world through the Rituals of Telepathy, and he longed to be a part of it. To laugh, to cry, to dine from sparkling dishes, to wait in line for a burger at the drive-thru behind the wheel of a shiny, yellow convertible. Although the jungle and the clan were all he knew of home, a thoroughly human yearning for freedom often overwhelmed him. He knew that he was a slave, regardless of the fact that the chimps, ironically, deferred to him. Most decisions regarding Double V had to be cleared through him. And although he'd spent his entire life among chimpanzees who had no more clue as to the identity of their fathers than a puddle can reconstitute itself into its individual raindrops, and therefore had no concept of fatherhood nor loyalty therein, Envee-vee still felt a fierce devotion to his own biological father, Vic the Elder. He was willing to do anything to get his attention and make him proud. If only he could manipulate his own rise to power rather than use a hairless chimp as a puppet, he was certain his Dad would look up from the *Wall Street Journal*, wink and smile. Although he had not had direct contact with a human being since his mother swaddled him in wet blankets and set him in that willow and pitch basket when he was two months old, in Envee-vee's heart of hearts he knew that he was a real Thorn. In his heart of hearts, he was a staunch conservative.

*

Gambo-bo was seething. Why was Envee-vee insisting that they spend so much time and energy on this tax cut?

"Us gots **a foreign-handed foreign policy** what is belligerent and militerroristic," Gambo-bo screeched. "Us am getting into trouble with Chinese, Russianese, Iraqese, Koreanese, Afghanese, Francese, and whatallese, and people wants to shoot, stab, or strangulate us. The demonumentalization of wildlife refuges is going smoothfully, the stuck market is falling and pensions are unappearing. Us is helpful of environment pollutenators and is dessicating the air, water, and earth. We are smallening big government and giving control to big business. We ignored ten million peace protestants, including the Pope and the Daily Lama. We still haven't found any weapons of massive destraction.

We've undecreased the national debt by millions of billions. Everything is going great! So why is you wasting away on this tax cut?" Gambo-bo bounced around the cave, shaking with anxiety, teeth bared.

Envee-vee was nonplussed, continuing to dismember a bright orange and black butterfly. "I'm running the chimp for re-election. With Double V's global popularity polls showing him down in the single digits and Michael Moore's attempts to convince working class Republicans and dissatisfied non-voters to go Democratic, I've got to do something to make the folks at home happy." And in his mind he thought: "I've got to make sure that the throne is still there when I get to it."

"If this am the best humans can do, chimps'll be in controlship of this planet in six months," spat Gambo-bo. "There won't be more need of elecutions."

"Relax, Monkey Boy. The tax cut meets all the criteria for your chimpanzee agenda: it distracts attention from our activities of destabilization and destruction, it inspires people to shake off their frugal reactionism to the economic recession and spend their money—I shudder to use the word—*liberally*. Once they get another taste of purchase power, they'll lose their resolve and want more, more, more. The whole plan is backloaded so that the real cost to the taxpayer doesn't come due until my two terms are up. The rich get richer, the poor grow more despondent. I'm telling you, this tax cut is a masterpiece."

They were interrupted by a knock at the entrance of the cave. A couple of bright-eyed chimps poked their heads in. "Sorry to bother you, Envee-vee, us is just come under for a couple sacks of the pre-shredded salad mix."

Envee-vee looked up from his work. "What do you have to offer in trade?"

"Figs!" said the first, displaying her armload, jumping up and down with excitement.

"Sap!" said the other, sticking out her goo-saturated arm triumphantly. Envee-vee sighed. "I'll take the figs, but the fruit flies better be fresh."

The chimps scooped up a sack of dismembered insects, left the figs, and hunkered back into the evening. "Thanks, my 'panzee," they called over their shoulders.

"My 'panzee my butt!" sniffed Envee-vee.

Gambo-bo was disgusted. "Me am unbelieving that you is able to sell insects which any chimp can find no cost all the anytime."

"Anyone can *find* insects," smiled Envee-vee, "but not everyone can *market* them."

*

President Thorn swung from the chin-up bar in the oval office, watching himself on the evening news with his press secretary, Gail Reese.

"And so I hope that everyone will run out and spend your tax refund and help simulate our economy!" he grinned into the camera. **"It's your money. You paid for it."**

"Let's take a little trip across America and see how folks *are* planning to spend their checks!" came the chipper voice-over as the camera settled on one modestly dressed middle-aged white woman.

"I'm hoping to get my electricity turned back on," she told millions of listeners. "Between my company downsizing and the power rates doubling, I just haven't been able to keep up."

A tall young African-American man said, "That check is going to help my Mama get new uppers, you know, dentures. Hers broke over three months ago and Medicare doesn't cover replacements. She says she's gonna gag if she has to eat another banana."

A distinguished looking gentleman in a herringbone tweed sport coat lowered a cotton mask from over his mouth and nose before speaking into the microphone. "Well, I've developed these environmental allergies, which my HMO doesn't cover. I'm going to spend the money on a visit to a homeopath. Blargghhechh . . . " He began coughing and sputtering, and quickly snapped the mask back in place.

"I'm going to buy a water filtration system. My little girl has leukemia, and we think it might have to do with the water quality."

"I'm sending it to the Sierra Club to help save the Arctic Wildlife Refuge!"

"I'm signing it over to Planned Parenthood."

"What tax refund? Whenever I get mail from the IRS I just toss it in the recycling bin."

"It's your money. You paid for it."

"I don't even think my *%#@+#*ing* fifteen dollar refund is going to do the economy any good. I can't even take my wife to the movies and pay for popcorn."

A thirty-something white man in a sharp business suit said, "I'm doing like Michael Moore and donating every cent to whoever can defeat Thorn in 2004!"

Cheering and hoots of approval rose from the crowd.

"What a surprise to run into former Secretary of Labor Robert Reich," said the shivering anchor woman. "Do you think Thorn's tax cuts are a good way to stimulate the economy?"

"I say, invest in job skills, public transit, and health," said Reich. "Let's call this 'bubble-up' economics. It empowers people to be more productive. It gives them a stake in economic growth. It is the only supply-side growth theory worth considering."

Back in the Oval Office, Double V grabbed his remote and changed the channel to a special report detailing the efforts of Bill Gates Sr., Steven Rockefeller, Warren Buffet, George Soros, and over a hundred others to oppose the repeal of the estate tax. Their new organization was called Millionaires against Tax Cuts for Millionaires.

Double V clicked off the TV. "You little ungrates," he spat, fuming at the blank screen as if it were the face of the American people. "I am the most powerfullest person on this planet! I can step on you like a little ant. I can step on the whole planet and turn the Arctic into a greenhouse."

"Victor, let's get back to your calendar," urged Gail Reese. "Friday night, the 27th, we're planning an emergency cabinet meeting to discuss our continued denial of accusations that we are prematurely pulling out of Iraq for political reasons, and our media plan to downplay the resentment and outrage we are attracting worldwide. After that, we're meeting with the Joint Chiefs to finalize plans for the defense missile testing."

"July 27th!" screeched Double V. "No way. No can do."

"But Mr. President, these issues are absolutely crucial."

"On the 27th, *Planet Of The Apes* opens, and Mom and I already have tickets. See if the Veep can cover for me."

*

If absolute power corrupts absolutely, then the illusion of power runs a close second. Despite the best efforts of the Poobahs to control his every move, as the weeks and months ticked along, Double V seemed ever more possessed by some unrecognizable force, and the Grand Ol' Poobahs had to reel in even more of the little bit of slack they had granted him.

"I am mindful of the difference between the executive branch and the legislative branch. I know the difference, and that difference is they pass the laws and I execute them," he told the press. "And that's what I'm for: more executions."

Double V continued, a wild look in his eyes. "When I was the guv of a big state, we boasted more executions per year than any other state. And that included lots of persons who were considered legally mental retards. Now that I'm prez of a big country I want as many executions as possible. **This has had full analyzation and has been looked at a lot. I understand the emotionality of death penalty cases.** My emotionalities on the issue are high! Why we have to pay room and board for a bunch of thugs and bad guys is unsensical and makes no sense whatever."

His ideas grew more and more bizarre. He wanted to open all national parks to oil drilling, timber sales, and coal mining, while sanctifying zoos as national monuments. He wanted to speed up the greenhouse effect and begin immediately developing banana plantations, engaging members of the Pacific Green Party as indentured servants. He promised, if re-elected, to convince the European Union to become an outlying suburb of Pittsburgh.

"They want the federal government controlling Social Security like it's some kind of federal program? Well here's what I suggest. At age sixty-five, the poorest eighty percent of the population play a little game of Russian roulette. Them that survive will be happy to live slightly above the poverty line." Thorn chuckled. "Eeee eeee, eeee, just kidding on the square."

Gail Reese turned to him in shock. "Sir, did you say kidding on the square?"

"Yes I did. It means I'm just kidding, but I really mean it. Eeee, eeee, eeee!"

"But President Thorn," continued Reese, "that term was coined by Al Franken, and he is devoted to dethroning—I mean, getting you out of the White House!"

Double V dismissed her concern with a wave of his hand. "He also writed in his book that I'm charming, and everything I say gives him the willies. Willies are good, isn't they?"

Most bizarre, perhaps, was his insistence on advancing a new weapons technology even though the other super-powers, intent on stabilizing peace, feared that he was starting a new arms race. He explained, **"It's important to think beyond the old days of when we had the concept that if we blew each other up, the world would be safe."** Thorn wanted to start testing the new missiles as soon as possible.

Among themselves, the Poobahs said, "Vic, we can't let him talk anymore. Our own party loyals are jumping ship. Tell him he's going to have to read from scripts. Too much bad media. He's out of his mind."

Vic the Elder protested, "But we control the media! Remember a few years back when we got them to continuously report that the press was in the hands of liberals? They'll say anything we want."

But Double V finally went too far. "Look, the bald eagle is practically instinct, so what kind of symbolization does that offer our great nation? I am bringing it up to Congress, and I'm sure they'll approve—because they always kiss my butt—that we change our natural symbol to the greatest creature of all—the chimpanzee!"

Even the reporters were rendered speechless.

"And while we're at it, it's time we changed the name of the Republican Party to an even honester name: the Imperial Party! And to add to its greatness, there will be a silent *Ch* at the beginning, to honor our new national symbolistication."

The (Ch)Imperial Party? "It is the Year of the Monkey," Vic the Elder offered feebly, just before he relented. "Boy," he said, "we've got you some new speechwriters. We're not going to let you ad lib anymore."

*

Envee-vee dropped the praying mantis he was dismembering. A cold chill ran through him. It was time to make his big move.

CHAPTER ELEVEN
OUT OF AFRICA

On a windless night, when the moon was dark and the beasts and bugs were snug in their burrows and the jungles and grasslands were motionless as a painting, Envee-vee noticed a strange sound in the distance. He could not place it immediately: A gathering storm? A stampede of rhinos? (*Good,* he thought, *my rhinoskin toga is worn pretty thin.*) An earthquake? A nightmare? And then he realized what it was—chainsaws. Later, as he entertained himself via mental games on the long journey across the ocean, he was able to retrace the trail of the emotional pinball that the sound of distant chainsaws set in motion within him:

1) Mortal fear—our home will be destroyed. Which gave way to—

2) A wave of pure pleasure: our plan for destroying the environment is working. Which gave way to—

3) Confusion. Why did the chimps want to destroy the environment in order to take control of the planet and thus protect the environment? Which gave way to—

4) Loyalty. He hoped Dad was getting a cut of the profits from destroying the rainforest. Which gave way to—

5) Greed. What would his share of Dad's profits add up to? Which gave way

to—

6) The ecstasy of redemption: Where you find the weapons of destruction, you can also find a ride back to the factory. Cool!

It didn't take Envee-vee long to put his plan into action. He had no bags to pack, no farewells to bid. As long as he laid off picking the lice from his dreadlocks for a few days, he'd have plenty to eat for the trip. What he did need to do was to move swiftly, yet naturally, and not arouse any suspicion among the members of the clan.

He high-tailed it off in the middle of a stormy night when the wind was howling so loud that the jackals couldn't hear themselves pray. He had not a tear in his eye. He was going home!

After several days bushwhacking he arrived at the lumber camp. The sound of the chainsaws was deafening. He quickly chewed some dry grass into wads and fashioned a pair of earplugs. Then he climbed into the branches of a tall, densely leafed tree to survey the situation.

The view from the tree limbs caused another series of emotions to pinball through him. The sight of the decimated forest—thousands of years of complex growth laid waste like a war zone in which both sides had lost, the stumps bare as amputations oozing sap—filled him with horror. The sun blazed, burning his sensitive eyes. No bird could be seen. Nearby, a beetle scurried in confusion. He popped it into his mouth. How could the conservatives permit, indeed encourage, such deforestation?

Then he was overcome with a wave of guilt, for doubting, even momentarily, the veracity of the conservative agenda. Profit was sweet, whatever the cost, of this he was sure. He came not to judge, but to escape. And having read, by means of the Rituals of Telepathy, many dozens of times, the Curious George books, he knew exactly what to look for: a man with a yellow hat. That man would be his ticket out of Africa.

After spending the night in a makeshift nest in the crook of the big tree, and guzzling a nice big handful of fresh-squeezed leaf dew, Envee-vee found what he was looking for—not one man in a yellow hat, but dozens of them. Not tall sombrero-style hats like the one the man in the Curious George books wore, but hard round hats that the men seemed to need to protect their delicate heads.

As long as he laid off picking the lice from his dreadlocks
for a few days, he'd have plenty to eat for the trip.

His first impulse was to rush out, pump one of the workmen's hands, and tell him his whole story—though he had helped direct speech towards some of the most powerful people on the planet, he'd never actually talked to one before. But he swallowed his baser instinct. These African workers were the lowest of the low, pawns in the multi-nationals' global scheme and unworthy of his attention. He needed a ride to America. He needed to talk to the Grand Ol' Poobahs. He wanted his mommy.

Still, Envee-vee observed with amazement and envy the men chatting easily with each other, throwing their heads back and laughing, slapping each other on the back, wiping the sweat from their brows with the backs of their sleeves. What a great idea! Envee-vee made a mental note to try it out as soon as he acquired a sleeve.

One by one the chainsaw motors cut off, and the men began to gather. Envee-vee sensed a certain excitement in the air, and heard, in the distance, another unfamiliar sound. It seemed to be motorized, not unlike the chainsaws, but of a deeper timbre. And then he saw a cloud of dust rise up from out of the now barren land.

It was a fleet of flatbed logging trucks come to take the timber to the coast, load it on massive ships, and carry it to the U.S.

Envee-vee again acted by dark of night, fitting himself into a niche on the loaded bed of the lumber truck, surrounded by cushions of long grass and soft leaves. It would be a long trip, but he was confident of its outcome. He closed his eyes and began to plan what he would say to Dad, Mom, Jab, Nill, the Grand Ol' Poobahs. They'd be so excited to see him and lose that hairless chimp! Of course, he'd keep Vee-vee with him as a sort of pet because, although they'd never met, they were like brothers: his own mother had raised Vee-vee, and Vee-vee's mom had raised him. He dreamed about the taste of mesquite-smoked beef tenderloin and pecan pie with vanilla ice cream. He wondered about the taste of broccoli— why did Dad hate it so much? He imagined how it would feel to choke on a pretzel.

Unbeknownst to Envee-vee, in the deepest dark of the night and very close at hand, another stowaway tossed a knapsack of Blue Manna into a cozy niche on another lumber truck, adjusted vines with the dexterity of a master puppeteer and the skill of a chimp who had been weaned to a joystick and could manipulate reality using as little wrist as possible. Gambo-bo, too, settled down for the long journey.

CHAPTER TWELVE
FIRST CONTACT

As fate would have it, the tedious trip through mile upon day of splintery darkness, over land, across the sea, and over land again, deposited the pair at the most advantageous location possible: just outside the site where military engineers prepared the new anti-ballistic missile defense system for testing.

When he was certain that the last worker had gone home, the lumber yard was empty, and the coast was clear, Envee-vee crawled out of his niche with a great Tar-AR-ar-AR-arzan-esque cry of joy. He filled his lungs with the sweet aroma of American air, bent over and kissed the ground. Since none but the single eye of the moon watched, he engaged in some interpretive dance, leaping from log to log, beam to beam, hood to forklift, expressing his sense of freedom and gratitude. The crickets chirped their accompaniment; Envee-vee reached down to munch a few. Then he made his way into the night, heading toward the lights of the test missile construction site.

Peeking out from behind a pile of rough hewn 2 X 4s, Gambo-bo observed him, undetected. The faintest hint of a smile crossed his lips. He grabbed his sacks of Blue Manna, and stole into the night.

*

The sound of cars and trucks rattling across the desert on their way to the test site woke Envee-vee out of a deep sleep. He watched as each vehicle arrived, stopped and the driver showed something to a uniformed man in a tiny house, then drove inside. Envee-vee felt a deep sense of calm; he would know when to make his move.

And then his moment of opportunity pulled up. It was an official bus filled with women and a few men decked out in business garb. He noticed when they stopped at the guardhouse that the luggage bins underneath the bus had been left slightly ajar. Silently, he crawled into one of them, and rode with the other important personages onto the site. Even more stealthily, Gambo-bo climbed into the other compartment.

It was a tour that had been arranged for spouses of United States senators. The women and men unloaded and gathered around a young man in military attire who informed them that he would be their guide.

After roughly outlining the schedule for the morning, he concluded by saying, "And after we explore the inner workings and top secrets of these weapons of mass destruction, we'll complete our tour with a nice long stop at the gift shop where you can buy miniature missiles and souvenirs to bring home to the kiddies."

Everyone chuckled politely.

It was then that Envee-vee made his move.

Because he had waited his entire life for this exact moment, it seemed to happen in slow motion. His earliest memories were of imagining this very instant, when he would speak to human beings and refer to himself by his rightful name. He envisioned their amazement, followed by the flood of relief that would wash over them: "We knew Double V had to be an imposter," they would sigh.

He crawled out of the luggage bin, stood erect. The group turned towards him *en masse*, sucked their breath in sharply, partly in amazement and partly because the stench was nasty. He opened his mouth. The words were as sweet as honey on his tongue. The eyes of the group widened in amazement.

"I," he said, his voice trembling, "am the real Victor Vincent Thorn, come to take my rightful place as President of the United States of America. The man

"*I am the real Victor Vincent Thorn, come to take my rightful place as President of the United States of America.*"

who now sits in the White House is actually a hairless chimp named Vee-vee who was switched at birth, and he is the pawn of the chimpanzees' scheme to take control of the Earth."

Although he spoke every word with pride and conviction, all that the people heard was "Oo oo, aa aa." They stared at him in horror and confusion. Envee-vee cleared his throat and tried again. "It is I who pushed this missile-defense plan through."

But, alas, all that came out was, "Oo oo aa aa."

Then everyone spoke at once, without ever addressing Envee-vee.

"It's Bigfoot!"

"Isn't he a legend?"

"How did he get in here?"

"I always thought he'd be bigger."

"Are we on *America's Best Top Secret Videos?*"

"Is he a mutant infected by living near nuclear seepage?"

"Are we at the right place—is this a movie set?"

The women instinctively clutched their purses; whether this was to beat him off should he attempt to hump their legs or to prevent him from stealing their wallets, they could not have said.

One man, sensing the photo opportunity, whipped out his digital camera and began taking pictures that would soon appear on the front pages of the tabloids.

Suddenly, a kind-eyed woman in a black dress dappled with animal fur, stepped toward Envee-vee with her palms open and facing outward the way you would approach a dog to let it know that you were friendly. She understood that he was trying to speak, although she couldn't understand him.

"You poor thing," she said.

It turned out that she was a veterinarian with a strong Dr. Doolittle streak; she was able, at varying levels of complexity, to communicate with most animals. She had healed malignant tumors by helping animals release the pain of being separated too early from their mothers. She had cured many a case of dog breath through intuiting minor dietary adjustments. She could get even the most secretive animal to reveal where Dad's car keys were buried in the yard.

She was a strong animal rights activist—not only wouldn't she wear fur or leather, but she would not wear silk, which was made, she declared, "by slave worms". She was a strict vegan, and kept a small menagerie at home.

She rooted around in her large purse and offered him first a dog biscuit, and then a banana.

"Take me to your leader," said Envee-vee.

But all that came out was, "Oo oo aa aa."

"Oh, I think he wants the banana," said the kind woman, beginning to peel it for him. "I'm taking him home with me. I'm not sure where he came from or what he is, but I want to try to figure it out before the authorities get to him and treat him roughly."

It turned out that the name of the kind woman was Dr. Jeffery, and she was the wife of the senator from Vermont.

When the bus pulled out through the gate, Envee-vee was in the back seat. Although the spouses were well aware of the racial/historical implications, they crammed themselves into the front few rows and opened all the windows.

When the bus pulled away, Gambo-bo was not on it.

CHAPTER THIRTEEN
MEETINGS WITH REMARKABLE CREATURES

The bus pulled into D.C., the scent of cigars and cherry blossoms filling the air. Envee-vee pressed his face up against the window in the same way that a child would in order to gross out someone on the other side of the glass. He did not do it to upset the pedestrians or drivers in the other vehicles; he was simply and powerfully drawn to the sights and scenes around him. Besides, he was a little near-sighted, and kept forgetting that the glass was there. He wanted to merge with the city, inhale the gas fumes, feel the concrete beneath his bare feet; he wanted to eat the leaves and flowers and insects, and gaze in awe at the Washington Monument as he slowly, sensuously licked cherry tree sap off his fingers. At this point, though, he was willing to eat the chrome off the fenders; he was starving. Although he instinctively felt that it was beneath his dignity to do so, he gobbled the dog biscuits, banana, sunflower seeds, millet, and everything else that Dr. Jeffery offered from her bag.

"The poor fellow's famished," she told the others. "Doesn't anyone have anything else to feed him?"

The women searched through their purses but didn't come up with much: a pack of stale cheese crackers, some honey-roasted peanuts from the plane, and a partially melted Snickers bar.

"I've got some diet pills," one woman offered. "You know, to take the edge off."

Dr. Jeffery insisted on taking him home in her SUV. "Don't worry. He won't be any problem. We have an understanding. Don't we, Sasquatch?"

"I'd like it if you could arrange for me to have a meeting with President Thorn and my father, Vic the Elder, as soon as possible. I have important information to share with them," explained Envee-vee, mustering as much urgency into his tone of voice as he could without seeming rude.

"Oo oo, aa aa," heard the senatorial spouses.

"Oh, he's frightened," said Dr. Jeffery, looking concerned.

She buckled him into the passenger seat and headed toward home, maintaining a running monologue along the way.

"After the hamsters there's seven dogs, if you count Lionel and Lila the pugs. Not everyone really thinks of them as dogs, they are kind of like large hamsters but not really. They're a little iffy with strangers, but I'm pretty sure they won't bite, if they do their teeth are so little I don't think it will cause a puncture wound, but they will be curious. See that red shiny thing? That's a traffic light; it means we have to stop. Oops, see that guy just ran the red light. Oh now see that spinning light and hear that siren? That's a cop. Oh look, that's the little market Thorn referred to as **'Hispanically owned'**. How did he make it through Yale? Of course we're Republicans on both sides of the family, always have been. So we're feeling torn about his plan to make the zoos into national monuments, I mean, as animal lovers we're for it, as Republicans, well, it's hard to know what to think. I mean, the (Ch)Imperial party, really. Look, here's our driveway."

She took him into a large bathroom, showed him how to work the faucets, brought him a bar of soap, a bottle of Kwell, a fine-toothed comb, a couple of oversized towels and—to replace the ragged rhinoskin toga—a navy-blue sweatsuit.

"Now, while you clean up, I'll feed the other animals and check my messages, change into some jeans, and then I'll be ready to really listen to you."

She closed the door.

For the first time in his life, he was alone in a room!

Envee-vee marveled at the shining tile, the soft rugs, taking in the view of

"You animal."

a pristine lawn while munching on the bar of soap. He played with the dials and flushed the toilet several times. He turned and shuddered with fear, before realizing that *he* was the man in the mirror. He contemplated his unwavering reflection for a long time. How different he looked from the other humans he'd seen, not only through Vee-vee's eyes, but now through his own. He definitely couldn't meet Dad looking like this.

Finally he drew a bath, entered with a deep sigh, soaked and scrubbed until his skin was red and tingly. He knew to dry himself with a towel, wrapping it around himself like a toga. Then he looked through the cabinets, found a pair of scissors and a razor blade, a can of shaving cream, and bottle of Brut aftershave. Carefully, with the precision of a man who had spent his life following the speech and actions of the President of the United States through the subtle manipulation of winged insects, he trimmed off his hair and beard.

"You animal," he growled, smiling at his reflection, and opened the door of the bathroom.

"You're a man!" gasped Dr. Jeffery. "Oh my God, I didn't, I mean . . . here, sit down, and tell me your whole story."

*

When she heard the sound of the electric door opener, Dr. Jeffery ran out to greet her husband in the garage.

"Honey, we have a very, well, unexpected visitor."

The Senator feigned anger, assuming that the "unexpected visitor" was of the furry, scaled, or feathered sort he'd grown accustomed to. "You haven't taken in another adorable homeless creature now, have you, dear?

"No, I mean that's what I thought at first, I wasn't really sure what he was, but well, actually, but . . . "

"Spit it out, dear. I've had a long day."

She decided to go for the punch line. "It's the President."

"Why, that overeager . . . I can't believe it! He's invited me over tomorrow to try and assuage my doubts about where he's taking the party, but I had no idea he'd come suck up to me in my own home."

"Well, it's not that President, I mean it is, but not the one you think. Oh!"

And she pieced together a thumbnail sketch, outlining their meeting at the missile test site and the salient information Envee-vee had revealed to her, and then dragged her disbelieving husband into the house.

Envee-vee squatted in the corner of the sofa, picking at the tiny threads in the loose weave of the upholstery. In the few minutes she was gone, he had almost completely unraveled the arm of the sofa.

He stood, embarrassed, reached out a hand in greeting. "Oops, nervous habit. I'm used to constantly pulling things apart," which of course came out, "Oo oo aa aa."

"Shake his hand, honey," whispered Dr. Jeffery, fumbling to make the proper introductions. "Senator Jeffery, this is, well, the real Victor Vincent Thorn."

Slowly, the senator put out his hand and said in the steady voice of a man who had learned long ago never to doubt his wife, "I'm pleased to make your acquaintance."

"Oo oo, aa aa," said the real Thorn, jumping and gesturing emphatically.

Dr. Jeffery translated. "He says since you are a Republican, you ought to be able to help him get a private audience with the President and his father as soon as possible."

Although the senator was always calm and collected, a good listener, and an excellent diplomat, he wasn't quite sure how to act. He had spent the day in private chambers with party leaders, bitterly deriding the President's policies both foreign and domestic. Since the Republicans held control of the Senate by a single vote and wielded that miniscule edge to ram their agenda through, they could not afford to lose him. And now, a man who resembled and sounded like a hairless chimp was in his house, in his sweatpants, pulling apart his sofa, and claiming that the President of the United States was actually a hairless chimp who had been switched at birth. It seemed so unlikely, and yet he trusted his wife and her intuitive gifts completely . . .

. . . and Double V *had* asked Congress to change the symbol of America to the chimpanzee. And one had to consider his mannerisms: that laugh—eeee, eeee, eeee—the jungle gyms, his inordinate fondness for bananas, his history of getting plowed on banana daiquiris. His reckless disregard for subject-verb agreement. It all started to make sense.

"You know, I've always wondered about Vic the Elder's V.P., Don Quill. Do you think it's possible that he is another chimp switched at birth? How about Raygun? Or Furred?" Senator Jeffery, with his wife as translator, sat with the real Thorn and talked far into the night.

"So it was his father, or uh, your father, who insisted that he act like he had a mandate?" inquired Jeffery, leaning forward.

"Oo oo, aa aa," yipped the real Thorn, barely able to contain his excitement.

"Honey, he says that Double V didn't even know what a mandate was until his S&L man explained it to him."

Well, thought Jeffery to himself, rubbing his mental hands together. *Come the dawn, I'll be pulling the plug on his little mandate.*

The very next morning he would arrive at the White House, his out-of-town guest in tow. Dr. Jeffery was scheduled for surgery—removing a Rolex from the stomach of a Golden Retriever—and would be unable to come along to translate.

CHAPTER FOURTEEN
REUNIONS

When the test site was quiet but for the sound of the night watchman jerking repeatedly awake at his station, Gambo-bo made his move. He could steal silently through leaf and banana peel muck; creeping across linoleum was a piece of cake.

The next time the watchman nodded out, Gambo-bo inched up on him, then swiftly and smoothly smeared Blue Manna on the backs of the guard's hands. Startled, the man opened his eyes, gazed in confusion at his iridescent knuckles and leapt into action, ready to attack.

Gambo-bo tilted his head to the side and grinned that sort of chimpanzee grin humans adore.

"Well, looky that," said the guard. "No one told me there was a monkey on site."

Gambo-bo lifted his right hand in a purposely clumsy attempt at waving hello.

"Aw, that's cute," said the guard, lifting his own hand and waving back.

Gambo-bo made the peace sign. The guard made the peace sign.

Gambo-bo beat his chest Tarzan style. The guard beat his chest Tarzan style.

Gambo-bo threw back his head and said, "Oo oo, aa aa." The guard threw back his head and said, "Oo oo, aa aa."

Gambo-bo placed his right hand on his left elbow and his left hand on his right elbow, squatted down and did a little jig. The night watchman placed his right hand on his left elbow and his left hand on his right elbow, squatted partway down, groaning, and did a little jig.

Gambo-bo slapped the back of his hand to his forehead in a gesture of mock despair. The guard did the same.

And as soon as the watchman made that gesture, smearing Blue Manna across his forehead, completing the trilogy of necessary placement and establishing his own enslavement, Gambo-bo reached into his sack and pulled out a length of jungle vine. "Eeee, eeee, eeee," he chuckled. "Now you is unslaved to me for all internity."

He began manipulating the guard like a marionette. After a few dramatic pirouettes and a "speak no evil, hear no evil, see no evil" routine for fun, he settled the guard into a chair in the corner of the room, and then sat himself down at the keyboard.

Of course, computers had changed a lot since Gambo-bo's days in the video game testing/military training lab, but the basic binary principles had remained the same. After several minutes, familiarizing himself with the program and hacking around, he was able to reset the monitors so that the actual missile test area was no longer displayed; he replaced those images with views of the vacant cafeteria and the empty space just behind the guard's chair. He explored for a while longer, making mental note of codes and information.

Then Gambo-bo returned the guard to his station, grabbed the sacks of Blue Manna, and slipped back into the night.

*

As Senator Jeffery and his now-suited companion strode across the White House lawn, the real Thorn argued a mile a minute.

"I'm really upset that you're leaving the party. I trusted you! I confided in you as one of my own! I feel terrible that my first influential act is to weaken the Republican base of support." Which the senator heard as "Oo oo, aa aa. Oo oo aa aa."

Senator Jeffery could tell from the real Thorn's tone of voice that he was upset. He said, "A lot of Thorns are angry with me. But the United States is being controlled by a bunch of chimpanzees and I'm the only one brave enough to put this monkey business to a halt."

"Oo oo! Aa aa!" screeched the real Thorn.

They turned the corner and came upon one of the elaborate jungle gym stations Double V had built when he first took office. Dozens of children swung nimbly, climbing upside down, laughing, calling out to each other, while parents snapped photos with disposable cameras. A wave of sadness washed over the real Thorn, a longing for home. Home? How absurd. *This*, he thought, *all this, is home*.

And then he spotted them, surrounded by bodyguards, heading out of a private entrance and into their limousine: former President Vic the Elder and Deedee Thorn.

Dad! Mom!

Although Dr. Jeffery had suggested that walking upright rather than knuckle-walking might help to make him appear more human, he felt the urgency of the moment, his opportunity slipping away, and began racing toward his parents on all fours.

The real Thorn began jumping up and down, waving and screeching, trying to get their attention.

"Oo! Oo! Aa! aa!"

The door to the limo opened.

Deedee Thorn put her hand to her breast—a gesture of calming herself, or of salutation?

The Secret Service agents placed their hands inside their sport coats and fixed their eyes on him. The real Thorn sensed that they were not about to do the Pledge of Allegiance.

Senator Jeffery chased after the real Thorn, grabbed him by the back of the suit jacket. "Oo oo! Aa aa!"

Where had Deedee heard those words before? For a moment, she gawked. Even from a distance, there was something so familiar about this fellow.

Dr. Jeffery had suggested that walking upright rather than knuckle-walking might help to make him appear more human.

Something so chimp-like.

Senator Jeffery called to the Secret Service agents, "He's with me. I'll deal with him."

They nodded without changing their stance.

Deedee got into the car after her husband. "Honey, I know you gave me a lot of flack for coming out pro-choice in my autobiography, but when you see poor creatures like that one, perhaps you can understand my position a little."

CHAPTER FIFTEEN
THE (CH)IMPERIALS

"It is clear our nation is reliant upon big foreign oil. More and more of our imports come from overseas." Double V stood, trembling, leaning over the large table, around which sat his staff and advisors. They all wore oversized nametags displaying their monosyllabic names: Bob, Bill, Joan, Dick, Jane, Spot, Dot, Carl, Cain, Sue, Chris, Lee, Paul Wolf, and of course, Dan Matt and Gail Reese.

"We've gotten unreliant on our own big oil! I say we have to rebegin anew by starting over at home. **Natural gas is hemispheric. I like to call it hemispheric in nature because it is a product that we can find in our neighborhoods.** So let's drill the heck out of our national parks, the wildlife refugees, our neighbors' backyards; who cares?!"

All around the table, people exchanged horrified looks: either he was back into the daiquiris, or the President had experienced some sort of mental breakdown. Gail Reese leaned over to Dan Matt, who had developed a nervous habit of pulling hairs out of his head whenever Double V spoke. Although Dan had a full head of hair when he first came to Washington, he was now almost completely bald.

"You have to start writing his remarks and responses even for private meetings," she whispered urgently. "We can't let him say anything anymore. His behavior is completely out of control."

"The rain in Spain falls mainly on the plain," responded Dan in a sort of Bela Lugosi voice.

"Don't joke, Dan," scolded Gail. "We're the tent poles holding up this whole circus."

"Mr. President," interjected Dan Matt. "Have you reviewed the speech I prepared for this afternoon's press conference?"

"No, Mr. S&L man, I have not viewed your nice little speech." He swung his arms out to the sides as if to wipe all the papers off the table, clear the slate, wipe away the past. It was an unfamiliar gesture, as were so many of his movements during the past few weeks.

"I am mindful not only of preserving executive powers for myself, but for predecessors as well. If I throw away my freedom to ad libs and extemporaryize on the spur of a moment, I am foreshortening my and they future. I'll be misspeaking whatsoever I want at that press conference this afternoon. **I know what I believe. I will continue to articulate what I believe and what I believe—I believe what I believe is right."**

Just then the door to the conference room opened and a Secret Service agent wheeled in the Vice President. He was surrounded by members of his staff, a nurse, and a priest.

Everyone looked up eagerly, as relieved greetings filled the air.

"Mr. Vice President, **it's just inebriating** to see you! It's been a long time since you were well enough to attend a meeting." Double V offered the V.P. his hand to shake.

The Vice President reached out his hand and opened his mouth to speak.

"I . . . *blergh ech hooey blaaaah!*" He doubled over, clutching at his heart.

"Oh my God he's having another heart attack!" Quickly the Secret Service agent, the staff members, nurse, and priest wheeled him out of the room.

There was a moment of silence in which Double V's staff and advisors drummed up enough courage to face the current crisis without the Veep's support. A collective sigh wafted into the air. Dan Matt began plucking at his eyebrows.

"Back to the agenda," prompted Gail Reese, the press secretary, who was dead set on changing the President's media image and thereby his poll ratings.

Double V bared his teeth. "Have we lost our hold on the media? They didn't report when those Swedians mooned me, they didn't report the teacher's union who opposed theirselves to my No Chimp, I mean, No Child Left Behind policy, they believed me when I said I had intelligence about weapons of massive distraction."

The Defense chair stood at his seat. "Mr. President, I don't think you are engaging the correct line of questioning here. What do you propose?"

"Because this is a **diplomatic nuanced circle**, I think I'm safe in saying that we have enough nuculer weapons to blow up the whole world about forty or twenty times. So I say let's go ahead and deploy those test missiles."

There was a knock on the door, and an aide stepped into the conference room. "President Thorn? Senator Jeffery is here for his meeting."

"Don't let him in!" Everyone present, save Double V, spoke in unison.

"I'll just step out and speak with him. Don't finishize any policies without me." The President grabbed a banana from the bowl on the table and headed for the outer room.

*

Senator Jeffery stood up, rejecting the offer of Double V's outstretched hand.

"Well, then. I think I know why I asked you here," began Double V accusingly.

"Sorry, Mr. Thorn, but you'll have to think again."

"And what if I don't want to?" snapped the president.

"I've received some information in the past twenty-four hours that will turn your pathetic presidency into history."

"I think we agree, the past is over." He slipped the banana from the skin and popped the whole thing into his mouth.

"Mr. President, what would you say if I told you that your every move was being executed by a power hungry chimpanzee?"

Double V worked his banana cheek to cheek, considered for a moment, and swallowed. "That's ridiculous. If I were being executed, I'd've been dead a number of times by now."

Senator Jeffery crossed his arms tightly in front of his chest. "This is no joke, Mr. President. A man claiming to be the real Victor Vincent Thorn showed up at my house and spilled the beans."

"Did he pick them up?"

"You're actually a hairless chimp who was switched at birth," continued the senator. "And now *I'm* switching . . . quitting the G.O.P., going Independent, and putting an end to your one vote lead and this whole monkey business. I will no longer support your simian policies. I'll fight you every inch of the way. It's over, finished, kaput."

"I guess you're telling me that a little banana plantation where Michigan used to be, farmed by indentured Greenpeace canvassers, won't help you change your mind?"

"Nothing will make me change my mind," insisted the senator.

"Well, then how can you be sure you got one?" The President tapped his chin thoughtfully. "Who have you leaked this story on?" he asked.

"Everyone; the *Post*, the *Times*, the *Herald*, the *Examiner*, the *Tribune*, CNN, AOL, NPR, ESP, PDQ, IOU, and the *Wall Street Journal*."

"Is anyone biting?" inquired the President.

Jeffery frowned. "No. Well, except the tabloids. By dinnertime tonight the story will be front page news in every supermarket checkstand in the country."

"Hmph!" exclaimed Double V. "Sticks and bones can break my stones but the tabloids isn't gonna hurt me. I'll tell you what, Jeffery, *if* I can still call you that. Go ahead and quit the (Ch)Imperials. We'll keep ramming our agender through just fine, within or without you."

Double V turned on his heel to leave. But just before he could open the door to the meeting room, the real Thorn stepped out of the shadows and met him face to face.

*

Meanwhile, at the missile site, Gambo-bo had completed his own switcheroo, deactivating the missiles and carefully filling them with shiny, iridescent Blue Manna.

Meanwhile, at the missile site, Gambo-bo
had completed his own switcheroo.

CHAPTER SIXTEEN
THE CHIMP WHO WOULD RULE THE WORLD

Double V and the real Thorn stared at each other, squinting, and then began circling around as if they were sitting across from each other on the Teacup ride at Disneyland, as if they were two gears in a well-oiled machine that never turned without affecting the position of the other.

"So, Monkey Boy," hissed the real Thorn, "finally we meet. My whole life has been handed to you on a silver platter—my parents, my birthday presents, my convertibles—but that hasn't stopped you from turning the whole shebang over to a bunch of demented chimps back in Africa."

But, as always, all that anyone heard was, "Oo oo, aa aa."

Now this alone was shocking enough to the receptionist and staff present who had not experienced the sound of the strange man's speech, but what came next was even more shocking, even to Senator Jeffery.

"**We spent a lot of time talking about Africa, as we should. Africa is a nation that suffers from incredible disease.** I've done my share. I gave at the office." The President spoke to this seeming lunatic as if he understood every word the strange man was saying! If Senator Jeffery had for a moment doubted the veracity of the real Thorn's story, all his doubts were now assuaged.

"You've been aware of your origins all along, haven't you?" the real Thorn asked. "Isn't it time to just give up the pretense and turn the throne over to its rightful inheritor?" Again, everyone else just heard, "Oo oo! Aa aa!"

"Don't try to trick me with your fancy words," said Double V. "I'll get my S&L man. He can translate anything into plain English."

"Oo oo, aa aa!" said the real Thorn.

"Well! I can reassure you that will be **in the *fore*thought of my thinking**," Double V countered sarcastically.

"Oo oo, aa aa!" growled the real Thorn.

"Don't bring my brothers into this," defended Double V. **"My little brother Jab, he's the governor of—I shouldn't call him my *little* brother—my brother, Jab, the great governor of Texas."**

"Oo oo! Aa aa!" spat the real Thorn.

"You're right. **Florida. The State of Florida."**

"Oo oo, aa aa? Oo oo aa aa?" asked the real Thorn.

"Will my memories of the future **become more few**? Will **war remain a dangerous place**? You ask some difficult questions that are answerless except by difficulter questions."

"Oo oo aa aa," said the real Thorn.

"I disagree with you," said Double V. **"I know the human being and fish can coexist peacefully."**

*

A huge storm was brewing, moving quickly and chaotically, a relentless wind that seemed to originate in all directions at once. The work crew broke down the outdoor set up and arranged for the press conference to take place inside. The President was furious about the change of plans.

"I told you I wanted NOT to do this in the House!" he fumed at Gail Reese.

"But, Sir, there's a hurricane-force storm heading in," she calmly explained, for the third time. "It is capable of damaging the microphones and equipment. There's lightning in the distance, which might knock out power, as well as endanger life and limb. It is highly likely that the reporters, if they stay, won't be able to hear you."

"Oo oo, aa aa."

"Tough tooties! I want to meet the press in the great outdoors."

"The work crew has already broken down the platform," countered Gail weakly.

"Well tell them to break it back up."

*

Two women in line at a Safeway spotted the cover story in the tabloids. The headline read: PRESIDENT ACTUALLY HAIRLESS CHIMP SWITCHED AT BIRTH. There was a photo of the real Thorn at the missile test site in his rhinoskin toga, his mouth puckered in an attempt at speech.

"Hmm, hmm," said the first woman, picking it up and flipping through to see more pictures. "My favorite one was when the lumberjack decapitated himself with a chainsaw but was saved by the miracle of microsurgery because his quick-thinking buddies put his head in an ice chest."

The second woman said, "I liked the one where the dad was reincarnated as the family dog and would help the kids with their homework." She grabbed the paper out of her friend's hands. "Well, if you ask me, I always thought he looked a lot like a chimp."

*

"There comes a time in the history of every great nation when you have to make yourself safe by making a lot of enemies," began Double V. "You have to move forward by taking a giant step backward. War and weapons is often the road we travel to rest in peace. There are **suiciders** out there. You can not make a stand while sitting still. "

All around the wind howled, and the rain dumped buckets on the shivering reporters in the bleachers.

"There's no question that the minute I got elected, the storm clouds on the horizon were getting nearly directly overhead. Who knows what a storm will bring–rain or sunshine? Sure, the folks over in Europe aren't liking my unitarianism, or unilaterality, whatever you call it. They don't like me testing anti-balsamic missiles. And it's just that kind of aptitude which can escalator into all heck breaking loose. Why sit back unprepared to blow up your latest enemies? To me **that's old, that's tired, that's stale. There may be some tough times here in America. But this country has gone through tough times before, and we're going to do it again."**

The reporters turned to look at each other. "Is he making any sense at all? It just sounds like 'oo oo, aa aa' to me."

A crack of spider web lightning momentarily illuminated the gloom.

All around the White House, the bushes caught fire and began to burn. Without changing his expression, Gambo-bo reached behind his ear for the joint he had been saving for just this occasion.

The bushes burned and burned. And they were consumed.

The President continued speaking into the microphone. "Oo oo, aa aa," he said. "Oo oo. Aa aa."

THE END
(hopefully)

SOURCES

Unless otherwise indicated, all quotes are from George W. Bush.

Chapter One: The Press Conference

"I don't want nations feeling like that they can bully ourselves and our allies . . . " and " . . . At the same time I want to reduce our own nuclear capacities to the level commiserate with keeping the peace." - Des Moines, Iowa (Oct. 23, 2000)

"We cannot let terrorists and rogue nations hold this nation hostile or hold our allies hostile." - Des Moines, Iowa (Aug. 21, 2000)

"We'll let our friends be the peacekeepers and the great country called America will be the pacemakers." - Houston, Texas (Sept. 6, 2000)

"First, we would not accept a treaty that would not have been ratified, nor a treaty that I thought made sense for the country." - *The Washington Post* (Apr.24, 2001)

"Russia should not fear the expansion of peace loving people to her borders." - Washington, D.C. (November 18, 2002)

"They misunderestimated me." - Bentonville, Arkansas, (Nov. 6, 2000)

"We're making the right decisions to bring the solution to an end." - Washington, D.C. (Apr. 10, 2001)

"Anyway, I'm so thankful, and so gracious—I'm gracious that my brother Jeb is concerned about the hemisphere as well." - Miami, Florida (Jun. 4, 2001)

Chapter Six: Hail to the Chief

"It's not the way America is all about." - Debate with Al Gore; Washington University, St. Louis, Missouri (Oct. 18, 2000)

"Well, I think if you say you're going to do something and don't do it, that's trustworthiness." - CNN online chat (Aug. 30, 2000)

Chapter Seven: Victor Vincent: The Early Years

"Republicans understand the importance of bondage between mother and child." - Okay, fine, this quote is from Dan Quayle

Chapter Eight: The Student Council Election

"What I am against is quotas. I am against hard quotas, quotas they basically delineate based upon whatever. However they delineate, quotas, I think vulcanize society. So I don't know how that fits into what everybody else is saying, their relative positions, but that's my position." - Quoted by Molly Ivins, *San Francisco Chronicle* (Jan. 21, 2000)

"I'm hopeful. I know there is a lot of ambition in Washington, obviously. But I hope the ambitious realize that they are <u>more likely to succeed with success as opposed to failure</u>." - Interview with the Associated Press (Jan. 18, 2001)

"The fact that he relies on facts—says things that are not factual—are going to undermine his campaign." *The New York Times* (Mar. 4, 2000)

"We ought to make the pie higher." - Columbia, South Carolina (Feb. 15, 2000)

Chapter Nine: Is Our Children Learning?

"The public education system in America is where children learn to take advantage of our fantastic opportunistic society." - Santa Clara, California (May 1, 2002)

"They said, 'You know, this issue doesn't seem to <u>resignate</u> with the people.' And I said, you know something? Whether it <u>resignates</u> or not doesn't matter to me, because I stand for doing what's the right thing, and what the right thing is hearing the voices of people who work." - Portland, Oregon (Oct. 31, 2000)

"Rarely is the question asked: Is our children learning?" - Florence, South Carolina, (Jan. 11, 2000)

"I will not stand for the subsidation of failure." - Florence, South Carolina (Jan. 11, 2000)

"When your teachers say, read— you ought to listen to her." - Washington , D.C. (Feb. 9, 2001)

"I read the newspaper." - In answer to a question about his reading habits, New Hampshire Republican Debate (Dec. 2, 1999)

"I want to thank the dozens of welfare-to-work stories, the actual examples of people who made the firm and solemn commitment to work hard to <u>embetter</u> themselves." - Washington, D.C. (Apr. 18, 2002)

"This is Preservation Month. I appreciate preservation. It's what you do when you run for president. You gotta preserve." - Speaking during "Perseverance Month" at Fairgrounds Elementary School in Nashua, New Hampshire; as quoted in the *Los Angeles Times* (Jan. 28, 2000)

Chapter Ten: Nature or Nurture?

"I will have a foreign-handed foreign policy." - Redwood, California (Sept. 27, 2000)

The quote, "Anyone can find insects. . .but not everyone can market them." is based on the quote from Andrew Pears, the founder of Pears Soap, who said "Anyone can make soap. Not everyone can market it."

"It's your money. You paid for it." - La Crosse, Wisconsin (Oct. 18, 2000)

"I say invest in job skills, public transit, and health. . ." "Let's call this 'bubble-up' economics. It empowers people to be more productive. It gives them a stake in economic growth. It is the only supply-side growth theory worth considering." - Robert Reich in *New Perspectives Quarterly*, (December 18, 2002)

"I am mindful of the difference between the executive branch and the legislative branch. I know the difference, and that difference is they pass the laws and I execute them." - Washington D.C. (Dec. 18, 2000)

"This has had full analyzation and has been looked at a lot. I understand the emotionality of death penalty cases." - *Seattle Post-Intelligence* (Jun. 23, 2000)

"They want the federal government controlling Social Security like it's some kind of federal program." - St. Charles, Missouri (Nov. 2, 2000)

"Kidding on the square." - Term coined by Al Franken in *Lies and the Lying Liars Who Tell Them: A Fair and Balanced Look at the Right*.

"But I also made it clear to [Vladimir Putin] that it's important to think beyond the old days of when we had the concept that if we blew each other up, the world would be safe." - Washington, D.C. (May 1, 2001)

Chapter Thirteen: Meetings with Remarkable Creatures

"A lot of times in the rhetoric, people forget the facts. And the facts are that thousands of small businesses—Hispanically owned or otherwise—pay taxes at the highest marginal rate." - Washington, D.C. (May 11, 2001)

Chapter Fifteen: The (Ch)Imperials

"It is clear our nation is reliant upon big foreign oil. More and more of our imports come from overseas." Beaverton, Oregon (Sept. 25, 2000)

"Natural gas is hemispheric. I like to call it hemispheric in nature because it is a product that we can find in our neighborhoods." - Austin, Texas (Dec. 20, 2000)

"I am mindful not only of preserving executive powers for myself, but for predecessors as well." - Washington, D.C. (Jan. 29, 2001)

"I know what I believe. I will continue to articulate what I believe and what I believe—I believe what I believe is right." - Rome, Italy (Jul. 22, 2001)

"It was just inebriating what Midland was all about then." - From a 1994 interview, as quoted in *First Son* by Bill Minutaglio

"You saw the president yesterday. I thought he was very forward-leaning, as they say in diplomatic nuanced circles." - Referring to his meeting with Russian President Vladimir Putin; Rome, Italy (Jul. 23, 2001)

"I think we agree, the past is over." - *The Dallas Morning News* (May 10, 2000)

Chapter Sixteen: The Chimp Who Would Rule the World

"We spent a lot of time talking about Africa, as we should. Africa is a nation that suffers from incredible disease." - Gothenburg, Sweden (Jun. 14, 2001)

"I want you to know that farmers are not going to be secondary thoughts to a Bush administration. They will be in the <u>forethought of our thinking</u>." - Salinas, California (Aug. 10, 2000)

[Then] Governor Bush: I talked to my little brother, Jeb—I haven't told this to many people. But he's the governor of—I shouldn't call him my little brother—my brother, Jeb, the great governor of Texas.
Jim Lehrer: Florida.
Governor Bush: Florida. The state of Florida. - From "The News Hour With Jim Lehrer" (Apr. 27, 2000)

"Will the highways on the Internet become more few?" - Concord, New Hampshire (January 29, 2000)

"I think war is a dangerous place." - Washington D.C. (May 7, 2003)

"These people don't have tanks. They don't have ships. They hide in caves. They send suiciders out." - Portsmouth, New Hampshire (Nov. 1, 2002)

"I know the human being and fish can coexist peacefully." - Saginaw, Michigan (Sept. 29, 2000)

"There's no question that the minute I got elected, the storm clouds on the horizon were getting nearly directly overhead." - Washington, D.C. (May 11, 2001)

"Russia is no longer our enemy and therefore we shouldn't be locked into a Cold War mentality that says we keep the peace by blowing each other up. In my attitude, <u>that's old, that's tired, that's stale</u>." - Des Moines, Iowa (Jun. 8, 2001)

"There may be some tough times here in America. But this country has gone through tough times before, and we're going to do it again." - Waco, Texas (Aug. 13, 2002)